Matins & Lauds, Prime, Terce, Sext, None, Vespers & Compline

The SelfScape Book of Hours

Auguste Rodin,
"Prodigal Son" or "Prayer"

Rainer Maria Rilke Edition

Selected Poems from Rilke's *Das Stunden-Buch* (*Book of Hours*)
and Excerpts from His Diaries and Letters,
Translated and Edited by Jeff Jinnett,
Illustrated with Images of Sculpture and Artwork
by Rodin, Barlach, van Gogh, Vogeler, Orlik, Kollwitz,
Cézanne, Modersohn, Kramskoy and Other Artists

Other Books by Jeff Jinnett:

The Seven Days of Creation: Poetry and Art Inspired by the Torah and Other Holy Scriptures (SelfScape Press 2015)

The Olive Tree in the Shadow of the Second Temple: Understanding Jesus the Christ through Second Temple Rituals and by Applying Scriptural Analysis Methods of the Jewish Sages to the New Testament (SelfScape Press 2015)

Translation, Introduction & Design Copyright 2018
by Jeff Jinnett
Published in 2018 by SelfScape Press
San Francisco, California

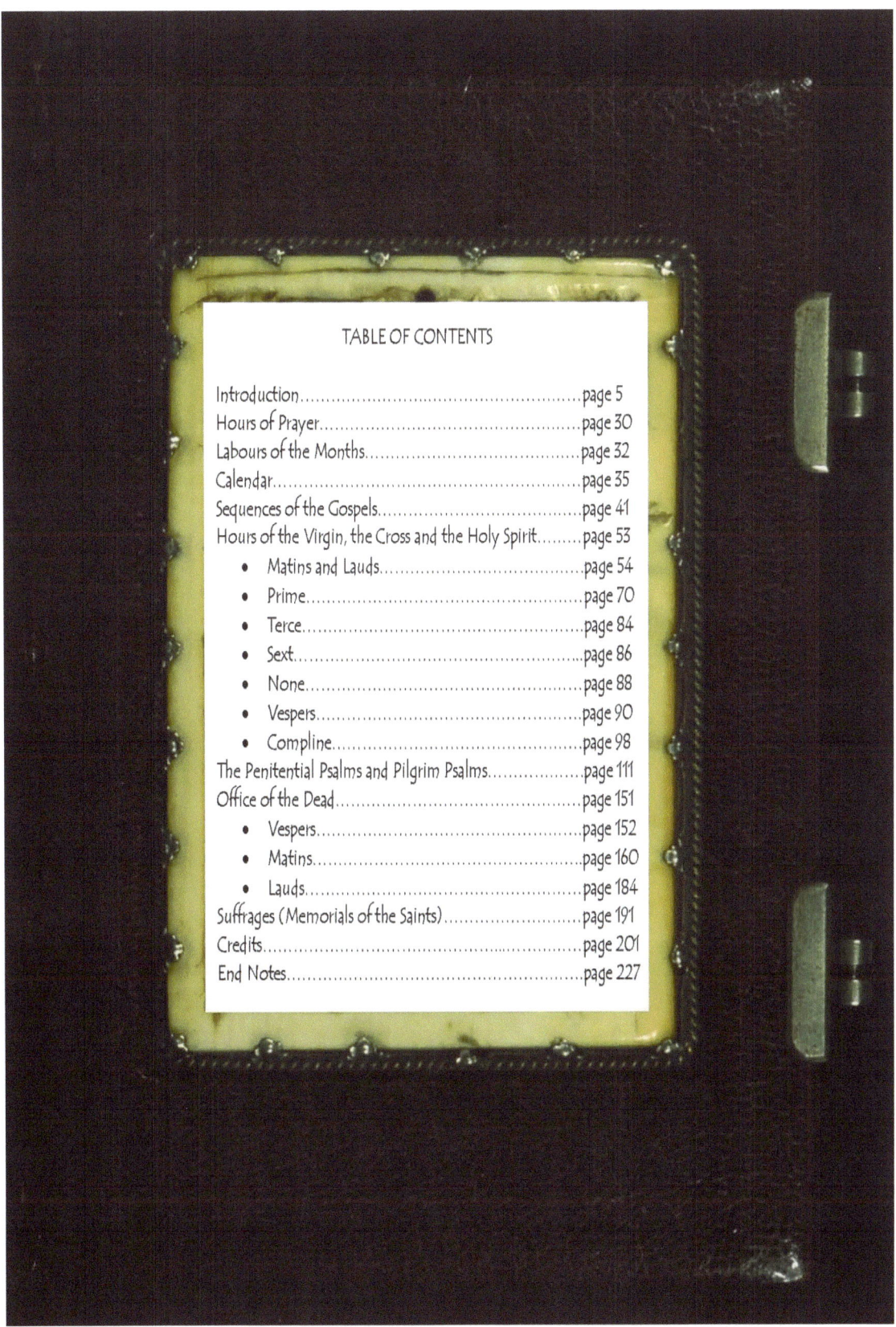

TABLE OF CONTENTS

Introduction	page 5
Hours of Prayer	page 30
Labours of the Months	page 32
Calendar	page 35
Sequences of the Gospels	page 41
Hours of the Virgin, the Cross and the Holy Spirit	page 53
• Matins and Lauds	page 54
• Prime	page 70
• Terce	page 84
• Sext	page 86
• None	page 88
• Vespers	page 90
• Compline	page 98
The Penitential Psalms and Pilgrim Psalms	page 111
Office of the Dead	page 151
• Vespers	page 152
• Matins	page 160
• Lauds	page 184
Suffrages (Memorials of the Saints)	page 191
Credits	page 201
End Notes	page 227

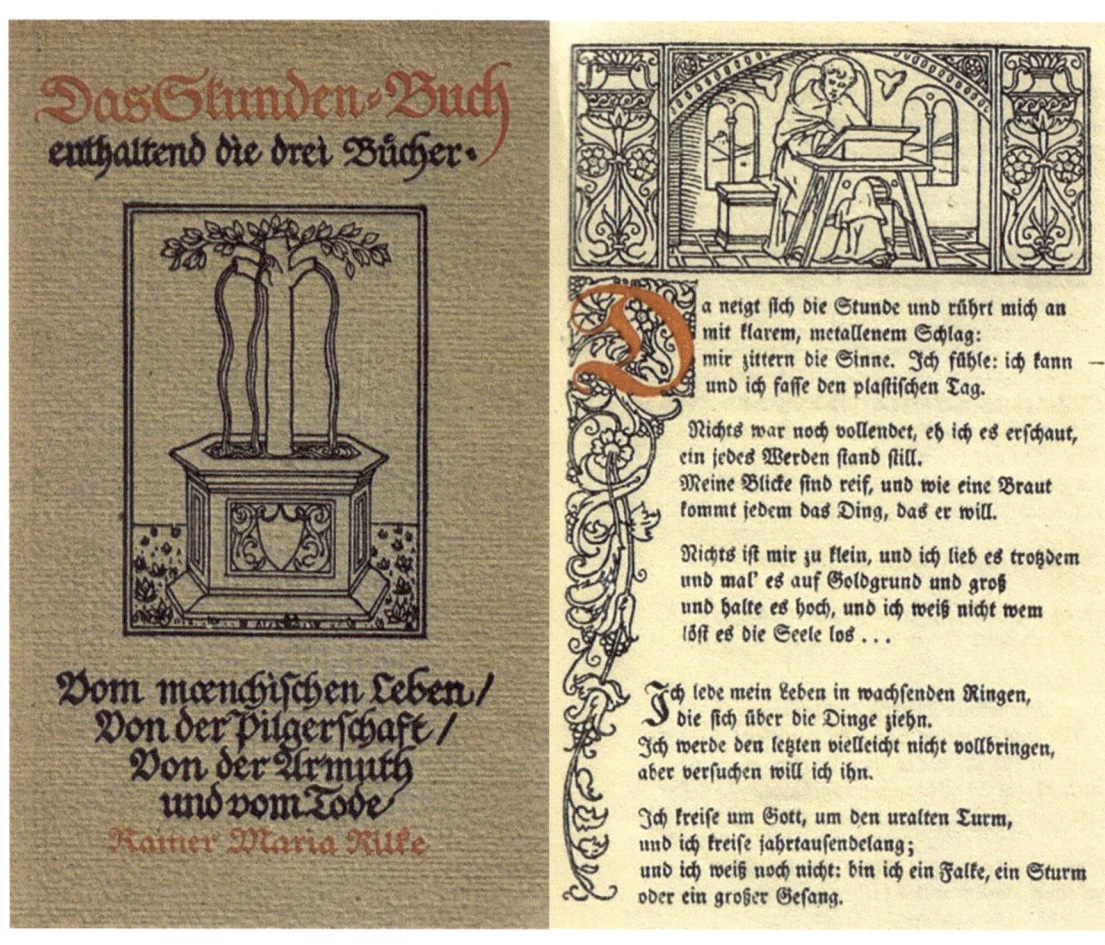

Rainer Maria Rilke, *Das Stunden-Buch*

(Front Cover and First Two Poems,
Illustrations by Walter Tiemann)

Introduction

"…you showed me your small evening drawings, and I feel with more than a growing realization from each black and red sketch – it must be that only the truest art done in the deep hours could have fulfilled what was in these sketches…Then I thought: Sometime I would like to have hours like these pages. Dark, and even more clear, with rich, countless things and figures, surrounded by beautiful patience. Now I know that I am living for such hours, for such poems."

–Letter of Rainer Maria Rilke to the artist Otto Modersohn, 23 October 1900[1]

Rainer Maria Rilke has been acclaimed as one of the most lyrically intense poets in the German language and he remains popular today, especially due to his later works, *Sonnets to Orpheus* and the *Duino Elegies*[2]. Rilke also was a prodigious letter writer and collections of his letters remain popular, such as his letters to Franz Xaver Kappus, a young man who wished to be a poet. These letters were published after Rilke's death as *Letters to a Young Poet*. The singer-artist Lady Gaga has a quote from *Letters to a Young Poet* tattooed on her inner arm and quotes from *Duino Elegies* and *Sonnets to Orpheus* still pop up occasionally in movies, television shows and novels. However, during Rilke's lifetime, his early work, *Das Stunden-Buch (Book of Hours)*, was the subject of public readings by Rilke[3] and others[4] and at the time of Rilke's death was considered to be one of his most important works[5]. This volume is dedicated to showing why Rilke's *Book of Hours* is a work of genius, deserving of further study.

Rilke's contemporaries viewed his *Book of Hours* to be a deeply religious work. The German poet Hans Bethge confirmed this in his 1909 review:

> "Rilke's book of poetry entitled "Das Stundenbuch" ("The Book of Hours") follows the "Book of Pictures". This beautiful and pious livre d'heures was published by the Insel Verlag in Leipzig in charming garb: it is printed by Drugulin on his Van-Gelder paper and illustrated with a pair of drawings by Walter Tiemann. The devotional book falls into three sections: 'On Monastic Life', 'On Pilgrimage' and 'On Poverty and Death'. These works are like running streams in open meadows at night; they seem to have no beginning and no end, they are sweet, melodious whispers of the secrets surrounding God. The works are touched by the beating wings of wonderful prophesy; here is a stammering dedication to the divine; humility and a deep faith; poignant poetry filled with images and visions that all lead to God."[6]

Another reviewer, Julius Bab, wrote in 1910 of Rilke that:

> "Rilke is a Christian of truly medieval proportions: one to whom God is all and the world nothing but a brightly colored hieroglyph for his holy name, and whose whole life is only a wistful searching through things to the actual, essential, highest … But whatever one may call it: in the mass of these verses is the 'Book of Hours', this stirring stream of prayer, this thousand-fold variation on the name of God, this solution of all temporal form in God."[7]

But were these reviews an accurate portrayal of Rilke's own religious beliefs? Born René Maria Rilke on December 4, 1875 in Prague (at that time located in Bohemia, part of the Austro-Hungarian empire), Rilke was raised as a Catholic by a very devout mother. Rilke took a Bible with him on his travels[8] and authored many poems inspired by the Bible – books such as *Life of Mary* and *Visions of Christ*, together with a slew of individual poems about Biblical figures such as Joshua, Saul, Elijah, the Prodigal Son, Lazarus, Saint Christopher, Saint Sebastian and others[9]. Nonetheless, even a cursory reading of Rilke's *Visions of Christ*[10] and his diaries and letters provides ample evidence that Rilke's personal religious views would have been thought highly unorthodox by his contemporaries, if known.

However, Rilke withheld publication of his *Visions of Christ* during his lifetime[11] and his diaries and letters also were not available publicly until after his death. Therefore, to understand Rilke's *Book of Hours* as his contemporaries did, we need to put aside what we now know from resources not publicly available at the time. Also, however unorthodox Rilke's personal religious beliefs may have been, his idiosyncratic search for God throughout his life cannot be underestimated. Thus, in a 1921 letter, five years before his death on December 29, 1926 from leukemia, Rilke writes:

> "First one has to find God somewhere, experience Him as so infinitely, so vastly, so enormously present; that whatever one feels toward Him – be it fear, be it astonishment, be it breathlessness, be it finally love – it really hardly matters. But religion - a coercion to God - there is no place for that if one has started with the discovery of God; there is then no stopping any more, no matter at whatever point one may have begun." –RMR Letter to Ilse Blumenthal-Weiss, 18 December 1921[12]

In part due to the central role images of nature play in Rilke's *Book of Hours*, it still resonates with today's reading public. For example, the Anita Barrows and Joanna Macy translation of Rilke's *Book of Hours* adopted an approach that emphasized the elements of nature in the book, while de-emphasizing the religious themes of the book.[13]

The *SelfScape Book of Hours: Rainer Maria Rilke Edition* takes a different approach in order to provide an understanding as to why Rilke's contemporaries viewed his *Book of Hours* to be a deeply religious work and not a paganistic ode to nature. Rilke's contemporaries were likely much more Biblically literate than today's readers and more familiar with the structure and purpose of a medieval Book of Hours. The choice by Rilke of the title "Book of Hours" probably was quite thought-out and deliberate. Although not known to his contemporaries, we now know that the work at its inception had the title "*Die Gebete*" – *The Prayers*.

Did Rilke change the name of the work to *Book of Hours* prior to publication in order to take advantage of his readers' familiarity with medieval Books of Hours? Certainly, the vellum-like paper chosen for the book, the illuminated first letter of the first poem and the accompanying image of the monk writing at his desk evoke the look and feel of a medieval manuscript. We also know from Rilke's letters that he had a fascination with the Middle Ages[14]:

> "… This last week I was in the Bibliotheque Nationale [in Paris] from 10:00 AM to 5:00 PM every day and read many books and saw many reproductions of cathedrals from the twelfth and thirteenth centuries…that was great, great art. The more one examines its creations, the more deeply one can appreciate the value and magnificence of the work; for these cathedrals, these mountains and mountain ranges of the Middle Ages, would never have been finished if they had had to depend solely on inspiration for their creation. Hand had to be applied to work day after day, and if each day wasn't an inspiration, still each was a path to it." Letter from RMR to Clara Rilke, 16 September 1902[15]

The Bibliotheque Nationale in Paris at that time had a collection of over 300 Books of Hours[16]. Since Rilke wrote that he had "read many books" including books on cathedrals of the 12th and 13th centuries, might he have seen some of the Books of Hours in the library's collection and been inspired by them to later reconfigure *Die Gebete (the Prayers)* into his *Das Stunden-Buch (Book of Hours)*?

Indicating a continued interest in medieval Books of Hours, Rilke noted in a 1906 letter to his wife Clara that he visited the Condé castle in Chantilly and saw Jean Fouquet's miniatures (Legends of Christ and the Saints)[17] taken from the Book of Hours of Étienne Chevalier, Treasurer to King Charles VII of France.[18]

And we know from a 1912 Rilke letter that the 14th century "always" had been the "most remarkable era" for him:

> "I marvel, am amazed at this fourteenth century, which always has been the most remarkable era for me, so exactly the opposite of our own time…[that] world, in which the Great Death [the Black Plague] of 1348, intoxicated by so much existence, no longer could control itself and invaded." - Letter of RMR to Lou Andreas-Salomé, 1 March 1912[19]

We now know that the original draft of *Die Gebete (The Prayers)* was annotated by Rilke to make a Russian monk named Apostol the protagonist or "voice" of the poems[20]. Some commentators therefore treat Rilke's *Book of Hours* as if Apostol, the poet-painter monk from the Monastery of the Holy Physicians ("Kloster der heiligen Anargyren")[21], were the protagonist throughout the entire book. However, Rilke's contemporaries did not know that the *Book of Monastic Life* originally was based on a fictional Russian monk named Apostol. Indeed, the *Book of Monastic Life* includes poems about the Virgin Mary, a poem where Abel is speaking about Cain and a poem where the speakers are cathedral builders, which would have encouraged readers to imagine other Biblical figures being the subjects of the poems, rather than just a single monk.

Therefore, the *SelfScape Book of Hours* does not confine the poems to one voice. Instead, consistent with Rilke's diary entry quoted at the beginning of this introduction, it envisions that Rilke's poems relate to "rich, countless things and figures", based on the Biblical figures which would have been the typical subjects of a medieval book of hours. In order to bring life to this concept, images of artwork by artists known to Rilke and his contemporaries are juxtaposed next to each poem selected from Rilke's *Book of Hours* to indicate a possible Biblical "voice" or figure for each poem. Rilke's

Leonid Pasternak, "Rainer Maria Rilke in Russia"

contemporaries may have instinctively attributed the poems to different Biblical figures in order to make the poems more accessible and understandable. For example, who is the "voice" behind the following poem from Rilke's *Book of Hours?*:

> What will you do, God, when I die?
> When I, your jug, lie broken?
> When I, your drink, am spilt?
> When I, your human cloak and craft –
> your earthly sense – am gone?
>
> Lost with me –
> the home that greets you,
> with words both close and warm
> I am the velvet sandals
> then dropped from your weary feet.
>
> Your great robe,
> fallen from your shoulders.
> Your gaze, which touched my cheek,
> warm as a kiss,
> will come, will search for me, long,
> only to find unfamiliar stones,
> lifeless in the lap of sunset.
>
> What will you do, God? I am troubled.

The poem could be interpreted in two ways – since it is in a Book of Hours, a devout reader might imagine that it is Jesus (God's "human cloak and craft" and "earthly sense") on the Mount of Olives as he prays to God, knowing that he is to be crucified. Since Rilke thought of artists as helping to create an "unfinished" God, it could be the poet expressing concern as to who will help express the inexpressible majesty of God once the poet dies. For purposes of this volume, the poem was paired with Albrecht Dürer's etching of Jesus praying at the Mount of Olives to illustrate what Rilke's contemporaries migh have imagined for the "voice" of the poem. We have to recognize the creativity of Rilke's poem, however, that it could be interpreted in both ways, with Jesus or Rilke (or an unnamed poet-painter) as the poem's "voice".

Once freed from limitations based on insider knowledge not known to Rilke's contemporaries, we again can ask: why did Rilke change the name of his book from *Die Gebete (The Prayers)* to *Book of Hours?* Is it possible that Rilke took the structure of a medieval Book of Hours, created poems that fit within that structure, and then deconstructed it in order to create his own uniquely personal Book of Hours? The answer to that question requires a short exploration of the history and structure of a medieval Book of Hours.

Book of Hours of Francois I, King of France
(Paris, France ca. 1532)

The Medieval Book of Hours

In the Early and High Middle Ages (5th century to ca. 1250 AD), Breviaries[22] or prayer books for monks were hand-made and illustrated on vellum, for use in reciting the liturgy of the hours. Traditionally, monks (such as monks belonging to the Order of St. Benedict) recited prayers seven times a day in order to comply with Psalm 119:64 ("Seven times a day I praise you for your righteous ordinances")[23]. Based on the Roman manner of time-keeping, these prayers were said at dawn, at the first, third, sixth and ninth hours of the day, at sunset and at bed-time. These times were called by their Latin names: Lauds, Prime, Terce, Sext, None, Vespers and Compline. In order to comply with Psalm 119:62, the monks also prayed at midnight ("At midnight I rise to praise you"). These "nocturnes" became known as the Matins prayers and sometimes Matins and Lauds were prayed together. Instead of a day beginning at dawn, the day for a medieval monk began at midnight and ended when he went to bed the following night. Matins was the first canonical hour[24].

At the beginning of the Late Middle Ages (ca. 1250 AD), a new shortened form of Breviary was created that was designed for use by lay people rather than monks – the Book of Hours. Rather than be a substitute for attending services in Church, the Book of Hours was intended to support the devout user in private prayer alone at home. The Book of Hours allowed lay people to participate in a more personal worship of God, without the intermediary of a priest. Books of Hours by the fifteenth century had become "the late medieval best-seller"[25] and were being mass-produced in workshops in cities such as Paris and Bruges by lay scribes and artists. Usually written in Latin, they ranged from simple prayer books for the middle class to very elaborate ones for the aristocracy and royalty, with artwork miniatures, initial letters illuminated with gold and silver and jeweled "treasure bindings"[26]. Although a medieval Book of Hours could be highly personalized to suit the preferences of the workshop creating it or the desires of the purchaser, most Books of Hours were variants of the following structure[27]:

1. Calendar[28] and Labours of the Months[29]: a calendar of important Church feasts and Saints' days, usually accompanied by artwork illustrating the "Labours of the Months" or activities typical for a rural society at every month of the year – e.g., hawking in May, harvesting hay in June and gathering acorns for the pigs in November[30]
2. Sequences of the Gospels: readings from the Gospels of Matthew, Mark, Luke and John
3. Prayers to the Virgin Mary (*Obsecro te* – "I implore thee"; and *O Intemerata* – "O matchless one")
4. Hours of the Virgin: prayers and chants relating to the life of Mary
6. Hours of the Cross: prayers and chants relating to the passion of Jesus
7. Hours of the Holy Spirit: prayers and chants relating to attributes of the Holy Spirit
8. Penitential Psalms (also known as the Psalms of Confession) and the Pilgrim Psalms (also known as "Psalms of Degrees" or "Song of Ascents"): Penitential Psalms (Psalms 6, 31, 37, 50, 101, 129, 142); Pilgrim Psalms (Psalms 120-134)[31]
9. Litany: after a three-fold call for mercy, *Kyrie eleison, Christe eleison, Kyrie eleison,* the Holy Trinity, Virgin Mary, Archangels and various Saints were invoked

10. <u>Office of the Dead</u>: prayers said for the repose of the soul of a decedent (not prayers from the Missal containing the Mass for the dead), plus readings from the Book of Job; recited only at Vespers, Matins and Lauds
11. <u>Suffrages</u>: Memorials about the lives of the saints

The basic texts found in each Hour (e.g., the Hours of Prime, Terce, Sext, etc.) included an opening verse and response, a *Gloria Patri*[32], antiphons[33], Psalms, and hymns[34]. The medieval Book of Hours typically had illuminated initial letters at the beginnings of prayers and contained artwork miniatures depicting Biblical figures as illustrations (e.g., the flight into Egypt for the Office of the Virgin, Christ on the cross for the Office of the Cross, King David to introduce the Penitential Psalms and Job on the dung heap for the Office of the Dead[35]). The *SelfScape Book of Hours* selects over 70 of the total of 120 poems from Rilke's *Book of Hours* and maps them against the traditional structure of a medieval Book of Hours, accompanied by images of sculpture, paintings and bas reliefs[36].

Rilke's *Book of Hours* is divided into three parts: the *Book of Monastic Life*, the *Book of Pilgrimage* and the *Book of Poverty and Death*. The poems from the *Book of Monastic Life* map well against the sequences of the four Gospels and the story arc of the birth of Jesus by the Virgin, his ministry and crucifixion, his resurrection and the descent of the Holy Spirit on Mary and the Apostles as contained in the Hours of the Virgin, Hours of the Cross and Hours of the Holy Spirit. Sometimes these Hours were combined as "mixed Hours"[37] and that is the approach this volume has taken. Poems from the *Book of Pilgrimage* evoke the tone of the Penitential Psalms[38] and Pilgrim Psalms[39] from a medieval Book of Hours. Poems from Rilke's *Book of Poverty and Death* resonate with the medieval Office of the Dead[40]. However, Rilke expands on the Office of the Dead by talking not only about actual death, but about the poverty he witnessed during his stay in Paris, which is a form of death in life. Rilke explained in one letter that the poverty and suffering he witnessed in Paris reminded him of the 30th chapter of Job – the book from the Bible traditionally read as part of the medieval Office of the Dead:

> "…the carriages drove straight at me, full of disdain, as if driving over a bad place in which stale water has collected. And often before going to sleep I read the thirtieth chapter of the Book of Job, and it was all true for me, word for word." – Letter of RMR to Lou Andreas Salomé, 18 July 1903[41]

Rilke also believed that one needed to accept death as an essential part of life and endure and come to an understanding with death, an attitude that was common in the Middle Ages, but not common in Rilke's time:

> "…by regarding God and Death as not having presence in Life (as being otherworldly, coming later, existing elsewhere, different), one has hastened the shrinking of the cycle of the here and now even more; this so-called progress became the happening of a self-impressed world which had forgotten that, already from the start, it was surpassed by Death and by God, no matter how hard it tried… Nature does not accept this somehow successful displacement of ours - when a tree begins to bud, Death blossoms within it as much as Life. The fallow field

is full of Death, having cast off its rich expression of Life, and the animals walk patiently from one to the other. All around us, Death is still at home, and from within the cracks of things it observes us, and a rusty nail, somewhere protruding from a board, does nothing but rejoice over it day and night." Letter of RMR to Lotte Hepner, 8 November 1915[42]

Rilke's final poems from the *Book of Poverty and Death* about Saint Francis of Assisi represent a counterpart to the Suffrages (Memorials of the Saints) from a medieval Book of Hours[43]. During his stay in Italy, Rilke sometimes met in the early morning at his lodging with other travelers to read to them from a book of stories about Saint Francis and his fellow monks – *The Little Flowers of Saint Francis*.[44] Rilke's poems about Saint Francis are juxtaposed in this volume with artwork by Eugene Bernand from that book. Rilke did not create any poems based on the prayers directed to the Virgin Mary or based on the Litany section of the medieval Book of Hours, because those sections included pleas for God's mercy and for Mary and the saints to intercede with God or Jesus on behalf of the user of the Book of Hours. This concept ran totally counter to Rilke's belief in having direct communion with God, without the intermediation of anyone.

A close reading of Rilke's *Book of Hours* indicates that his poems in each of the three parts generally proceed from night to day and end at night, as the prayers in a medieval Book of Hours would progress from Matins and Lauds (at night), to Prime, Terce, Sext and None (in the day-time) to Vespers and Compline (at night). Also, some of the poems appear to evoke the seasons, with the *Book of Monastic Life* sounding the notes of Spring and Summer, the *Book of Pilgrimage* presenting images of Autumn and the *Book of Poverty and Death* representing the season of Winter.

The *SelfScape Book of Hours: Rainer Maria Rilke Edition* therefore adopts the following structure:

1. Hours of Prayer: one poem from *Book of Monastic Life*
2. Calendar and Labours of the Months: one poem from *Book of Pilgrimage*
3. Sequences of the Gospels: selected poems from *Book of Monastic Life*
4. Hours of the Virgin, the Cross and the Holy Spirit (combined together as "mixed Hours"): selected poems from *Book of Monastic Life*
5. Penitential Psalms and Pilgrim Psalms: selected poems from *Book of Pilgrimage*
6. Office of the Dead: selected poems from *Book of Poverty and Death*
7. Suffrages (Memorials of the Saints): selected poems from *Book of Poverty and Death*

As with a medieval Book of Hours, the poems within the Hours of the Virgin, the Cross and the Holy Spirit are allocated among the Hours of Matins and Lauds, Prime, Terce, Sext, None, Vespers and Compline[45], progressing from night to day and then to night. Since the Office of the Dead only was recited at Vespers, Matins and Lauds[46], the poems for that Office are allocated among those three Hours.

Leaf from a 15th Century Book of Hours

Once we see the structure of a medieval Book of Hours underlying Rilke's *Book of Hours*, the brilliance of Rilke's deconstruction of this model in order to create his own personal Book of Hours becomes apparent. The medieval Book of Hours was designed for a devout user to pray to the Virgin Mary and the Saints to intercede on their behalf with God, to help them emulate the lives and virtues of the Saints and to remember the dead. Rilke's *Book of Hours* had a different point of view. Rilke's poems envisioned God as not being found within churches or in painted icons. Instead, Rilke's God came to those who thirsted for Him in solitude. God was not to be found in the cities, but rather in nature, where the flight of the birds and the waving of tree branches in the wind taught the soul how to move. In essence, Rilke envisioned poets and artists as merging God with their own creations and helping God to be fulfilled. Rilke described this in a letter written during his first visit to Russia in 1899:

> "I noticed it first in Moscow: this is a land of the unfinished God and the warmth of His becoming flows out like an infinite blessing from the gestures of the people" – RMR letter to Emil Faktor, 3 June 1899[47]

Rather than focus primarily on the afterlife (as was the case with a medieval Book of Hours), Rilke's *Book of Hours* was focused on the here and now – ultimately on life, love and death. The *SelfScape Book of Hours* casts Rilke's poems back into the structure of a medieval Book of Hours. This will enable readers to grasp why Rilke's contemporaries saw what they wished to see – a truly devout Christian work – when in reality Rilke had used that structure to create a uniquely personal and unorthodox world where the poet is co-creator with an "unfinished" God[48]. The "voice" of Rilke's *Book of Hours* is not that of a Russian monk, but rather Rilke's own unique voice:

> "There is perhaps nothing so jealous as my profession; and not for me a monk's life within a cloister's community and isolation, but probably I must see that bit by bit I myself should grow into a cloister and stand there in the world, with walls around me, but with God and the saints within me, with very beautiful pictures and furnishings in me, with courts around whom pillars dance, with fruit orchards, vineyards and wells whose bottoms are not to be found." RMR Letter to Elizabeth and Karl von der Heydt, 11 December 1906[49]

One commentator saw a definite "thematic unity" in Rilke's *Book of Hours*:

> "*Das Stunden-Buch*, which grew interlaced between the two phases of *Das Buch der Bilder*, exhibits remarkable thematic unity despite the fact that it consists of three distinct cycles with their distinct histories and settings. Yet from the start this tripartite body of poems existed in Rilke's mind as a single lyrical evocation of the divine which von der Heydt had praised. *Das Stunden-Buch* appears as an artfully constructed mosaic, one of the most consistently shaped thematic architectonics Rilke has created, comparable only to his later work."[50]

The "thematic unity" that allows Rilke's *Book of Hours* to be seen as a "single lyrical evocation" is because it derives its underlying structure from the medieval Book of Hours.

Lou Andreas-Salomé

"Last Appeal…If you are venture freely into the unknown, you are answerable to no one but yourself; but in the event you bind yourself to another, then you must understand why I so tirelessly kept pointing you towards such an individualistic path to health…In your 'Songs of the Monk', at certain earlier times, the past winter, this winter, you stood before me healthy!...Do you perceive my fear and my agitation when you slip back again…And thus your figure – in Wolfratshausen still so dear and distinctly close to me - was more and more becoming lost to me like a small detail in a busy landscape – in a vast Volga landscape, as it were, and the little hut in it was not yours. I obeyed without realizing it the great plan of life…With profound humility I accept it: and know now with prescient clarity and call to you: follow the same path towards your dark God! He can give you what I no longer can do for you and for so long have not been able to do with full dedication: He can grace you with sun and maturity."

- Letter from Salomé to Rilke urging him not to marry Clara Westhoff, 26 February 1901[51]

"Gelegt in die Hände von Lou" – "Placed in the Hands of Lou"

The final key to understanding Rilke's *Book of Hours* is grasping the significance of Rilke's dedication of the book to Lou Andreas-Salomé on the back of the title page with the words "Gelegt in die Hände von Lou" ("Placed in the hands of Lou"). Rilke first met Salomé on May 12, 1897 in Munich, when he was 21 and Salomé was 36. Born in Russia, Salomé was beautiful and a noted philosophical essayist and literary critic. She also was the author of the novels *Ruth* and *Searching for God* and a work on Henrik Ibsen's heroines. Rilke became infatuated with her, as had Friedrich Nietzsche, Paul Reé and others in her life. Salomé was married to Friedrich Carl Andreas, a tutor of Turkish and Iranian in Berlin until 1903 and later a professor of Iranian philology at the University of Göttingen. However, Salomé's relationship with her husband, fifteen years her senior, had been platonic throughout their marriage – Andreas had stabbed himself in the chest and threatened to kill himself if Salomé did not marry him[52].

From May 31 – June 1, 1897, Rilke and Salomé took a two-day trip to Wolfratshausen, a small village south of Munich, and it was on that trip that the two likely first became lovers[53]. Salomé persuaded Rilke to change his first name from the French "René" to the more Germanic and masculine "Rainer" and began teaching Rilke Russian so that he could read Russian authors in the original. In April–June of 1899, Rilke accompanied Salomé and her husband on a visit to Moscow and St. Petersburg in Russia, where he met Leo Tolstoy and other artists and writers. Rilke again traveled to Russia, alone with Salomé, from May to August of 1900. This trip involved visits to many cities across the Russian empire, from Kiev to Moscow[54]. During his trips to Russia, Rilke experienced Easter celebrations at the Kremlin, saw the Cathedral of the Assumption (*Uspensky Sobor*)[55] in Moscow, visited the Pechersk Monastery of the Caves near Kiev[56] and interacted with a wide range of Russians from peasants to aristocrats.

Russia formed the backdrop for Rilke's creation of the first part of his *Book of Hours* – the *Book of Monastic Life*. This first section of the *Book of Hours* was created in Schmargendorf near Berlin, Germany in September – October of 1899, just after Rilke returned from his first trip to Russia. Rilke's relationship with Salomé broke off in 1901, however, when he decided to marry the sculptor Clara Westhoff over Salomé's objections. The second part of Rilke's *Book of Hours* – the *Book of Pilgrimage* – was written in September, 1901 in Westerwede, Germany (near the artists' colony of Worpswede and the city of Bremen), shortly after his marriage to Clara on April 18, 1901, but before the birth of their daughter Ruth on December 12, 1901. The third part of Rilke's *Book of Hours* – the *Book of Poverty and Death* – was written in April, 1903 in Veraggio, Italy, shortly after Rilke's first extended (and uncomfortable) stay in Paris. At this time, Rilke and Clara were living apart to pursue their separate artistic careers, but still remained emotionally close. Rilke and Clara later grew apart irreparably but could not divorce due to Rilke's status as an official (although non-observant) Catholic. Rilke's work was always his abiding first love, resulting in a failed marriage to Clara and making a life of secure familial happiness with any of his subsequent lovers impossible for him. As Rilke wrote in a letter to Franz Xaver Kappus which was later included in *Letters to a Young Poet*:

> "Investigate the reason that you are writing; test to see if it stretches out its roots in the depths of your heart, admit to yourself if you would die if you would be forbidden to write. This above all: ask yourself in the quietest hour of your night: must I write? Dig into yourself for a deep answer. And if you are able to answer this serious question without hesitation with a strong and simple 'I must', then build your life around this necessity" – RMR Letter to Franz Xaver Kappus,[57]

Although Salomé was never again to be Rilke's lover after their break in 1901, Rilke was able to reconnect with Salomé in June of 1903 and she remained his confidante for the rest of his life, exchanging numerous letters with him[58].

Here's the puzzle – Rilke kept the poems that were to become his *Book of Hours* secret from everyone except for Salomé and at times Salomé may have held the only copies of the poems[59]. When Rilke decided to organize the poems into a Book of Hours for publication in 1905, he had to retrieve the poems from Salomé. Given that Rilke and Salomé no longer were lovers, why did Rilke keep the poems secret to all except Salomé and dedicate his *Book of Hours* to her on its publication? To answer that question, we need to go back to how Rilke and Salomé first met. In 1896, Salomé's article *"Jesus the Jew"* was published in the *Neue Deutsche Rundschau* and Rilke read a copy of it shortly thereafter. In the article, Salomé wrote:

> "Once one would say flatly, 'all religions arise from the interrelationship between God and humanity'... By starting from the point of view of man instead of from God, one overlooks almost involuntarily the impact of Godhood on the believers... it can be, however, that a religious genius – as a result of a particularly auspicious coincidence of times, circumstances and historical coincidences – will go deep within his secret, individual self and then reaching out with his exceptional concept of God, he will create the essential expression of the divine in words and images, as in the work of a poet in whose highest artistic dream the highest religious dream of humanity has become in in its fulfillment at once tangible, plastic, encountered."[60]

Rilke wrote to Salomé seeking an opportunity to meet her, writing that:

> "I was like one, whose great dream was fulfilled for good and for bad, for your *Essay* mapped to my poems like a dream to reality, like a wish to its fulfillment."[61]

Why did Rilke dedicate his *Book of Hours* to Salomé, years after their parting as lovers? Perhaps because Rilke wrote his *Book of Hours* to fulfill Salomé's wish to see "the work of a poet in whose highest artistic dream the highest religious dream of humanity has become in its fulfillment at once tangible, plastic, encountered."

But was Rilke's dedication of his *Book of Hours* more than just an acknowledgment of his intellectual debt to Salomé and proof that he had fulfilled the wish expressed in her article? Perhaps Rilke's *Book of Hours* was also a deeply personal and meaningful gift of love to Salomé – just as it was a tradition for husbands in the Middle Ages to give a Book of Hours to their wives as a wedding present.[62]

Lou Andreas-Salomé, Rilke's life-long muse, although less emotional than Rilke in her letters to him during his lifetime, still reciprocated Rilke's symbolic marital tribute of *Das Stunden-Buch* in her own memoirs – her *Lebensrückblick* ("Looking Back on Life"):

> "If for years I have been your woman, it was because you were for me *the first real thing* in my life –body and humanity indistinguishable, an undeniable proof of life itself. Word for word, I could have declared to you what you said to me as a confession of love: 'You alone are real.' In this we were wed, before we had even become friends, and became friends hardly by choice but rather through a subliminally consummated marriage. Not as two halves did we seek completion in each other: our surprised, shuddering oneness recognized itself in an unfathomable totality."[63]

The following poem originally was written as a love poem by Rilke to Salomé[64], but later was included in his *Book of Hours*:

> Blind me - I see you still,
> hear you, even though made deaf.
> Take away my feet and mouth,
> and yet I run to give my oath to you.
> Break off my arms – I yet reach for you,
> my heart holding you like a hand -
> even if you stop my heart,
> my brain would beat instead,
> and if then you set my brain ablaze,
> I would serve you with my blood.

For Rilke's early 20th century readers familiar with the Bible, this poem may have reminded them of Solomon's *Song of Songs* from the Bible. Although the *Song of Songs* appear to be poems of love from a man to a woman on their surface, they traditionally are understood to be love poems addressed to God[65]. Rilke's poem, like other poems in his *Book of Hours*, can be understood in the same two ways and expresses two intertwined forces in Rilke's life – a personal search for and merging with God through artistic creation and the search for God through human love.

About the Illustrations

From 1895 to 1896, Rilke studied art history, among other subjects, in Munich and Prague and art continued to be important to him throughout his life[66]. Woodcut artist Emil Orlik (famous for woodcuts created during his visit to Japan) was a friend from Rilke's childhood in Bohemia. Rilke's stay in Italy from April – June 1898 as evidenced in his Florentine Diary[67] awakened his appreciation for artists such as Michelangelo. Rilke became acquainted with the works of artists such as Ivan Kramskoy and Alexander Ivanov as a result of his trips to Russia in 1899-1900. Rilke authored an essay on "Russian Art" ("Russische Kunst")[68] and personally collected Russian religious icons[69]. In 1902, Rilke wrote a monograph about the Worpswede artists' colony and the artists living and working there, such as Otto Modersohn and Heinrich Vogeler.[70]

Edward Steichen, "M. Auguste Rodin"

"I see in Rodin what that means to him, that what is his is always around him ... That is one of his secrets, or rather one of the pillars of his greatness... but above all is the work. What you feel about Rodin: his work is space, it is time and wall, it is dream and window, it is eternity ... *Il faut travailler toujours* ('we must always work') ... The other day, Saturday, he said that, and as he said it - so deeply convinced from the work- It was just as simple as a sound and a stirring of his hands."

- Letter from RMR to Clara Rilke, 18 September 1902[71]

After finishing the Worpswede monograph, Rilke met Auguste Rodin in Paris as a result of a letter of introduction to Rodin from Rilke's wife Clara. Rilke wrote a monograph on Rodin's sculptures and in 1905-1906 was a personal secretary to Rodin. Rodin had a major impact on Rilke's life, advising Rilke he must work, always work ("*Travailler, toujours travailler*")[72]. While living in Paris, Rilke became familiar with the works of Van Gogh, Cézanne, Manet, Picasso and other artists. Rilke wrote numerous letters to his wife Clara about Cézanne's works[73] and both Cézanne's paintings and Rodin's sculptures had a significant influence on Rilke's approach to art and poetry.

The purpose of this book is to take 21st century readers from today as much as possible back into the late 19th/early 20th century world of Rilke's contemporaries and into their mind-sets. Therefore, the images chosen to illustrate the *SelfScape Book of Hours* are of artwork by artists known and admired by Rilke (e.g., Rodin, Cézanne, Van Gogh, Ivanov, Modersohn, Vogeler, Kramskoy and Orlik) and by artists likely known to Rilke and/or his contemporaries (e.g., Barlach and Kollwitz). In addition, other images are included, such as images of pages from medieval Books of Hours.

Excerpts from Rilke's Diaries and Letters

Also included as annotations to some of Rilke's poems are excerpts from his diaries[74] and letters[75]. These excerpts can help to explain some of the hidden, deeper meanings within the poems. For example, rather than his *Book of Hours* representing a paganistic worship of nature, Rilke confessed in a letter to his wife Clara that in the writing of the poems, just as prophesy came over Saul, Rilke saw "not nature but the visions she gave me."

> "If I were to come visit you [his wife Clara and daughter Ruth], I also surely would see with new and different eyes the splendor of moor and heath, the birches and the vivid floating green of the meadows, and this transformation is something I have experienced fully and shared before in part of the Book of Hours; but nature was then still a general occasion for me, an evocation, an instrument in whose strings my hands found themselves again; I was not yet sitting before her; I allowed myself to be carried away by the soul that emanated from her; she came over me with her vastness, her grand, over-exaggerated existence, the way prophesy came over Saul; just like that. I walked about and saw, saw not nature but the visions she gave me."[76]

In a similar vein, Rilke sees elements of nature as having the ability to teach us something about being spiritual:

> "After the bustle of the city to see these high waiting woods again! How refined this stand of trees is, this calm. Bewildered by the agitated gestures of human beings, one comes to feel that there are only two related and great movements. The beating of wings of a bird high above and the swaying of the treetops. These two gestures are meant to teach your soul how to move." Rainer Maria Rilke, The Schmargendorf Diary, 7 April 1900[77]

In another letter to an acquaintance, Ilse Jahr, Rilke reveals his concept of the "darkness of God" and his search for God in creation, love and death:

> "I began with things, which were the true familiars of my solitary childhood, and it was already a big step forward that I managed, without anyone's help, to get close to animals…But then Russia opened up to me and gifted me with the brotherliness and the darkness of God, in whom alone there is fellowship. So I also named him then, the God who had broken in upon me, and I lived a long time in the anteroom of his name, on my knees…Now you would rarely ever hear me name him - there is an indescribable discretion between us - and where once was nearness and fusion, there stretch new distances, as in the atom, which the new science also envisions as a cosmos, but on a small scale. The comprehensible escapes and is transformed, one learns relationship instead of possession, and a namelessness arises that has to begin again with God in order to be complete and without excuse. The experience of feeling is supplanted by an endless longing for all that can be felt… the attributes of God are taken away and – being no longer expressible - fall back just to creation, to love and death…which took place again and again in certain passages in the Book of Hours - this ascent of God out the breathing heart to cover the sky, and his descent again as rain."[78]

Finally, the format of a medieval Book of Hours suited Rilke as a vehicle for his solitary communion with God, as Rilke confirmed in one of his diaries:

> "If God has given a law, then it is this: Be alone from time to time. For he can come only to a solitary one – or to a pair he can no longer tell apart." RMR, The Schmargendorf Diary, Night, 25 November 1899[79]

Bible quotations

Medieval Books of Hours contained Psalms, Gospel readings and other excerpts from the Bible such as from the Book of Job and I have included a few Bible quotations where it seemed helpful to add context to some of Rilke's poems. For example, in one poem Rilke speaks of the voice of the poor that sees the ocean and speaks to Daniel in his dreams. This obviously is a reference to Daniel 7: 1-10, where Daniel dreams that the winds of heaven churn the sea, four beasts come up out of the sea and the books of judgment are opened by the "ancient of days". While Rilke's contemporaries likely would have recognized this Biblical reference immediately, most of today's readers likely would not, so I have added the Biblical annotation.

Although Rilke was officially a Catholic, the Bible he took with him on his travels and relied upon was a Lutheran Bible. Medieval Books of Hours pre-dated the Protestant Reformation and were distinctly Catholic. However, given Rilke's mixed religious sources, I relied upon the Revised Standard Version of the Bible (2nd Catholic Edition)[80], since that version of the Bible is generally thought of to be reasonably acceptable to both Catholics and Protestants:

> "…the Revised Standard Version of 1946-1957 was becoming established and, in 1966, was accepted by Catholics and Protestants as a 'Common Bible'. It was the first truly ecumenical Bible and brought together the two traditions – the Catholic Douay-Rheims Bible and the Protestant Authorised Version."[81]

Also, the Calendar of Feasts at the beginning of this volume is derived from the liturgical calendar of the Personal Ordinariate of the Chair of Saint Peter[82], which has incorporated some elements of Anglican liturgy into the liturgy of the Catholic Church.[83]

On the Selection and Sequencing of Poems

The *SelfScape Book of Hours: Rainer Maria Rilke Edition* contains over 70 of the 120 poems contained in Rilke's original work. Some poems from *Das Stunden-Buch* were omitted because the thoughts expressed in them were repetitive of other poems included in this volume. Others were omitted because they were very long and would have impeded the flow from one poem to another. Some were omitted because, although poetically elegant, they were overly focused on the role of an artist or dealt primarily with events or points of interest from Rilke's travels. For example, one poem included in the original work described the Cathedral of the Assumption in Moscow (in Russian: *Uspensky Sobor*):

The sun seldom visits Sobor.
But like unfolding wings of gold
the emperor's door presses
up to the wall formed of figures,
the Madonna and the ancients.

And at the columns' edge,
silver-silent icons eclipse the wall,
their gemstones rising
like a choir, only to fall
back into the crowns,
holding more beauty than before.

And the Lady hovers there,
moon-pale face, like blue nights,
she who is your joy:
she who opens the gate,
she is the morning dew
on the field that blooms forever.

From the cupola,
your Son gazes down
and makes it all whole.

I look on in trepidation –
will you deign
to ascend your throne?[84]

Heinrich Vogeler, "Sommerabend" ("Summer Evening")

(Painting of a summer evening gathering in 1905 at Heinrich Vogeler's home "Barkenhof" of some of the artists from the Worpswede colony, including sculptor Clara Westhoff Rilke, wife of Rainer Maria Rilke)

As can be seen from the photo[85] in the End Notes of Uspensky Sobor today, Rilke has nicely captured the look and feel of the Moscow cathedral, but since it is not essential to the purpose of this volume, it was omitted. Also, with respect to the sequencing of the poems selected, I have tried as much as possible to maintain Rilke's sequence in which poems appeared. For example, in the Office of the Dead, the order of the poems about the poor is unchanged from their original order. However, in a few cases, I did change the placement of poems. For example, the very first poem in *Das Stunden-Buch* beginning "Da neigt sich die Stunde und rührt mich an" ("Now the hour strikes and moves me") has been shifted to later in the story arc of the Office of the Virgin, the Cross and the Holy Spirit.

Approach Taken to the Translation

All translations of Rilke's poems, diary excerpts and letter excerpts are my own. One of the difficulties in translating Rilke's *Das Stunden-Buch* is that the metre of the poems is primarily end-rhymed iambic pentameter or iambic tetrameter. The poems also include a very creative use of alliteration, internal partial rhymes, and even new word combinations coined by Rilke ("neologisms")[86]. None of these characteristics (although enchanting in the original German) can be duplicated in a translation into English without destroying the sense and flow of the originals. I therefore chose a free-verse approach to my translations and sought to follow Walter Benjamin's advice on what constituted a true translation, opting not to be held captive to Rilke's metre, rhyming scheme and other features:

> "…as regards the meaning, the language of a translation can – in fact must – let itself go, so that it gives voice to the *intentio* of the original not as reproduction but as harmony, as a supplement to the language in which it expresses itself, as its own kind of *intentio*… A real translation is transparent; it does not cover the original, does not obstruct its light, but allows the pure language, as though reinforced by its own medium, to shine upon the original all the more fully."[87]

At times in this volume, I have included quotes from Rilke's letters and diaries touching on the same themes found in the juxtaposed poems. My hope is that readers can see how my translations of the poems resonate with Rilke's tone and "voice" as revealed in his letters and diary entries. An example of this is an excerpt from Rilke's Worpswede Diary, written in 1900:

> "The sky was a soft gray, with a few bright rips and tears that allowed sunlight through to touch the land on all sides, far and wide. The distances were like biblical scenes with their mountains, groves of trees, and waterways…Of ordinary contour, not any particular locale, simply: the earth. The earth over which the peoples have been scattered like dust in a storm. The earth which is too vast for man in his wanderings, the earth which reaches to the skies and on the other side of the oceans past days and nights begins and grows again, this strange biblical earth, the earth which God still holds in his hands and whose beginning and end thus cannot be seen. The heath stood there black and lusterless, the grass trembling, soft as Japanese silk, metallic red was the mowed buckwheat field, the plowed land dark and heavy." - Rainer Maria Rilke, The Worpswede Diary, 1 October 1900[88]

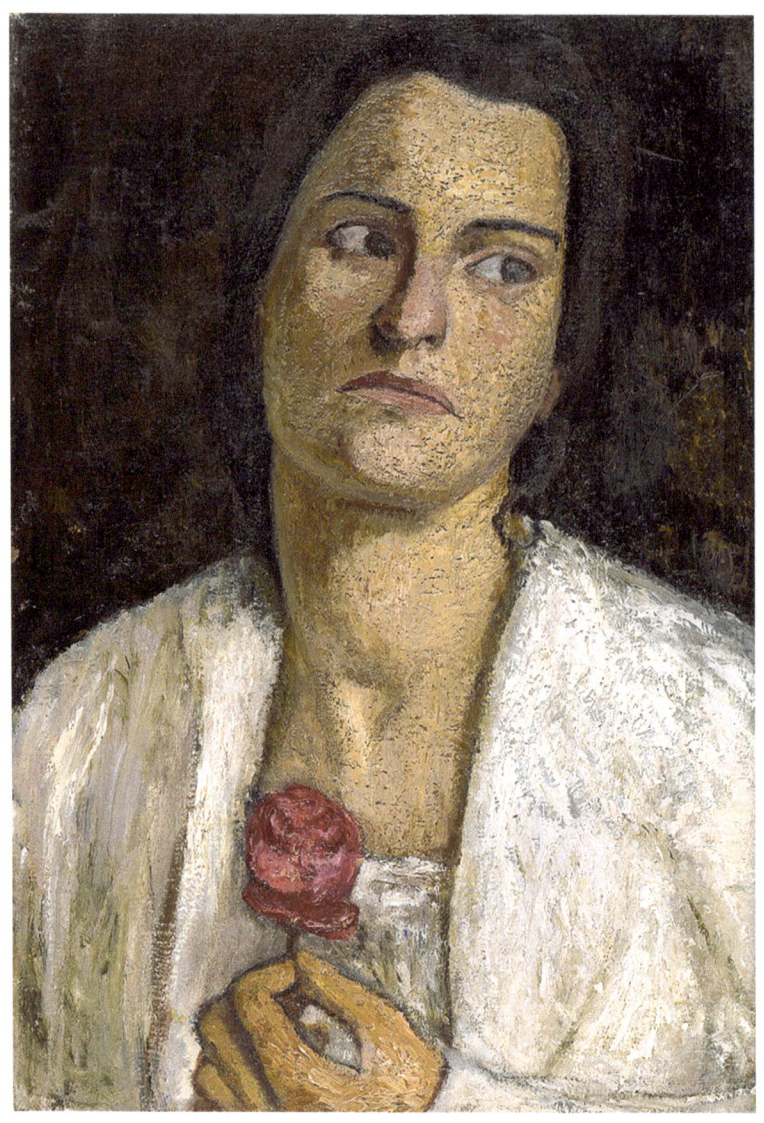

Paula Modersohn-Becker, "Clara Westhoff Rilke"

"That evening, as we sat together in the little blue dining room, we spoke also of other things: in the cottage there would be a light, a softly veiled lamp, and I would stand at my oven and prepare dinner for you…Red mandarins should be there, in which Summer is folded up very small like an Italian silk handkerchief in a nutshell. And roses would be about us, tall ones bending from their branches, reclining ones that gently raise their heads, and ones that wander from hand to hand, like girls in the pattern of a dance. So I dreamed. Premature dreams - the cottage is empty and cold and even my apartment here is empty and cold: God knows how it can be made habitable. But even so I do not believe that reality cannot reach some semblance of what I dreamed."

- Letter from RMR to his future wife, Clara Westhoff, 23 October 1900[89]

While trying to evoke the tone I found in Rilke's diaries and letters in my translations of his poems, I also adopted a translation approach based on Rilke's analysis of Cézanne's art, which Rilke admired greatly. Rilke felt that Cézanne's art was distinctive in its placement of colors next to each other, so that the colors (rather than the outlines of shapes) reacted to each other to create the ultimate work of art. Rilke noted this in his description in a letter to his wife Clara of Cézanne's portrait of Madame Cézanne, which Rilke saw in a Parisian salon:

> "Everything, as I have already written, has become a matter that is settled among the colors themselves: a color will come into its own and become dominant in response to another or recollect itself...weaker local colors will abandon themselves and be content to reflect the dominant ones. In this back and forth of mutual and varied influence, the essence of the picture vibrates, rises and falls back into itself, and does not have a single unmoving part...."
> – RMR Letter to Clara Rilke, 22 October 1907[90]

Also, here is Rilke's description of Cézanne's paintings *Still Life with Blue Blanket* and *The Sea at l'Estaque*:

> "On the other side, on the blue cover, some apples have rolled out partially from a bowl whose porcelain whiteness is determined by the cover's blue. This rolling out of red into blue is an action that seems to arise out of the interactions of the colors in the picture, much like the connection that arises between two Rodin statues due to their sculptural affinity. And finally a landscape of sky blue, blue sea, red roofs, communicating in green to each other and very involved in this mutual, inner conversation." – Letter from RMR to Clara Rilke, 4 November 1907[91]

I therefore sometimes treated Rilke's poems as if they were sliding tile picture puzzles, taking them apart and moving the pieces when necessary to allow the "weaker colors" to reflect the dominant ones. Then the poem in its entirety "vibrates, rises and falls back into itself, and does not have a single unmoving part". Thus, while trying to translate each poem as faithfully as possible, I at times simplified and altered the sequence of words, phrases and lines in order to more accurately express what I believed to be the true essence or *intentio* of the original poem.

For example, here is my fairly literal, line-for-line translation of a poem from the *Book of Pilgrimage*, with no alteration in the order of the images and no simplification of phrasing:

> Barberries now ripen into red,
> aged asters breathe weakly in their patch.
> Whoever is poor at summer's end
> will ever wait, having lost himself.
>
> He who now cannot close his eyes
> knowing that a wealth of visions
> only waits in him for the begin of night

> in order to rise up in his darkness: –
> it has passed by like an old man.
>
> They come no more, his days are gone,
> and all that happens to him, lies to him;
> also you, my God. Like a stone are you,
> that daily drags him into the deep.

Rilke opens the poem with two lines that evoke the colors of red and fading purple, with the red barberries almost ready to be picked by birds, so that the seeds can be spread far and wide. The fading purple of the asters makes it clear we are in Autumn. The next two lines present the figure of the poem, who is "poor" and sleepless, unable even to escape into his dreams. His days are gone, life for him is a lie and even God is like a stone that drags even deeper into his darkness. We now know that this part of Rilke's *Book of Hours* was written during a time when funds from Rilke's family had almost totally dried up and he and his pregnant wife Clara were living in a small peasant cottage and struggling financially.[92] This poem may well reflect Rilke's depression over his financial straits and the negative impact it was having on his ability to be creative.

But how would Rilke's early 20th century readers made sense of this poem as part of a Book of Hours, not knowing of Rilke's personal circumstances? The figure of the poem is not anyone seeking God and the "poverty" of the central figure may not be from a lack of material wealth. Now imagine the poem coming after the Spring and Summer story arc contained in the Hours of the Virgin, the Cross and the Holy Spirit. Just as the barberries must be eaten by birds and die in order for new barberry bushes to spread, the red of the crucifixion will lead to Christ's resurrection and the spreading of the "good word" by the Apostles throughout the world. The Apostles have been filled with the Holy Spirit and are spiritually "rich" at summer's end. There is one Biblical figure that the poem may have evoked for Rilke's contemporary readers – Judas Iscariot. For Judas, the thirty pieces of silver are worthless, he is sleepless with guilt and to him the thought of God indeed weighs him down like a stone.

With this Biblical figure in mind, here is my translation for this volume, with the sequence of phrases and lines reordered to have the "weaker colors" – the images of the barberries and asters – reflect the dominant one of the figure who is "poor at summer's end". I juxtaposed the poem against a sculpture of Judas, holding the rope he will use to hang himself and a sack containing his 30 pieces of silver.

> Whoever is poor at summer's end –
> as barberries now ripen into red
> and aged asters breathe weakly
> in their patch – will ever wait,
> having lost himself.
>
> He knows his wealth of visions,
> waiting for night's begin
> to rise up in his darkness,
> will pass by like an old man

> for eyes that now cannot close.
>
> His days are gone,
> no more than lies are left to him;
> to him, even you, God,
> are like a stone that daily
> drags him to the deep.

I have chosen to include Rilke's original poems in German side by side with my English translations, because any translation of a poem (including my own translation) cannot avoid becoming a new poem. For readers who are fluent in German, it always is better to read Rilke in the original German. Similarly, I have translated all included quotes from Rilke's diaries and letters but have included the original German texts as well in the End Notes.

Finally, I chose the title *SelfScape Book of Hours: Rainer Maria Rilke Edition* for this volume because I hope in the next few years to create a set of seven traditional Books of Hours devoted to the six days of creation, with each Book of Hours devoted to what was created at that day. The seventh Book of Hours for the day God rested would focus on the Church and be illustrated by images from stained glass windows and church sculptures. Whereas Rilke's *Book of Hours* is infused with beauty tempered by a solitary sadness as a result of his life, I hope this new seven-volume set will instead embody beauty and joy. These Books of Hours will include some of the traditional antiphons, chants, psalms and prayers that would have been found in a medieval Book of Hours, sometimes in both Latin and English. They also will include religious poetry and artwork appropriate for the particular day of creation. The first two volumes of the seven-volume set that are planned for publication are the following, for Saturday (when God created humans and beasts) and Sunday (God's day of rest):

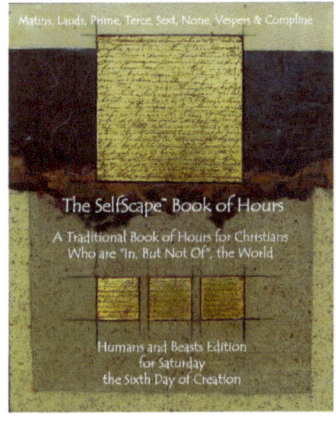 

Jeff Jinnett
San Francisco, California
August, 2018

HOURS OF PRAYER

Venetian Clock

Matins (Midnight)
Lauds (Dawn)
Prime (First Hour, around 6:00 A.M.)
Terce (Third Hour, around 9:00 A.M.)
Sext (Sixth Hour, around Noon)
None (Ninth Hour, around 3:00 P.M.)
Vespers (Sunset)
Compline (Bed-Time)

God, how do I know your Hours – you placed your words in front of you, so the Hours could round the space; the Nothing was for you like a wound that you cooled with the world. Now it heals softly among us. For us, the past is a calming pulse that we feel already as a gentle sway in the background, draining the fevers of the sick. We lie soothed on the Nothing, and we cover all the rips; but you grow into the unknown in the shadow of your countenance.	Gott, wie begreif ich deine Stunde, als du, dass sie im Raum sich runde, die Stimme vor dich hingestellt; dir war das Nichts wie eine Wunde, da kühltest du sie mit der Welt. Jetzt heilt es leise unter uns. Denn die Vergangenheiten tranken die vielen Fieber aus dem Kranken, wir fühlen schon in sanftem Schwanken den ruhigen Puls des Hintergrunds. Wir liegen lindernd auf dem Nichts, und wir verhüllen alle Risse; du aber wächst ins Ungewisse im Schatten deines Angesichts.

"At midnight I rise to praise you..."
-Psalm 119: 62

"Seven times a day I praise you for your righteous ordinances."
- Psalm 119:164

"This sacred seven-fold number will be fulfilled by us in this wise if we perform the duties of our service... at Lauds, Prime, Terce, Sext, None, Vespers, and Compline; and let us rise at night [Matins] to praise Him,"
- Rule of St. Benedict, Chapter 16[93].

LABOURS OF THE MONTHS

"Labours of the Months"
Lucy Faulkner Orrinsmith, Painter of Tiles, & Various Artist-Designers: William Morris, Edward Burne-Jones, Madox Brown, Dante Rossetti and Philip Webb

All will be great again and immense. Giant trees towering over low walls, waters rippling over open lands; and in the valleys, strong and diverse - a people of shepherds and farmers. Their homes all-welcoming, a feeling of sacrifice, unlimited, embraces you and me and all our interactions. And no churches that imprison God as one would a fugitive; then cry laments as if he were a wounded, caged animal. No waiting and looking for the hereafter - just the yearning to live in the earthly now, to be familiar to his touch, and not dishonor death.	Alles wird wieder gross sein und gewaltig, die Lande einfach und die Wasser faltig, die Bäume riesig und sehr klein die Mauern; und in den Tälern, stark und vielgestaltig, ein Volk von Hirten und von Ackerbauern. Und keine Kirchen, welche Gott umklammern wie einen Flüchtling und ihn dann bejammern wie ein gefangenes und wundes Tier, – die Häuser gastlich allen Einlassklopfern und ein Gefühl von unbegrenztem Opfern in allem Handeln und in dir und mir. Kein Jenseitswarten und kein Schaun nach drüben, nur Sehnsucht, auch den Tod nicht zu entweihn und dienend sich am Irdischen zu üben, um seinen Händen nicht mehr neu zu sein.

"For everything there is a season,
and a time for every matter under heaven."
- Ecclesiastes 3:1

"...try to love the questions themselves but love them as if they were locked rooms and books written in a very foreign language. Don't search now for the answers, which could not be given to you, because you would not be able to live them. The point is to live it all. First, live the questions. Then someday - far in the future perhaps - you will gradually, without every noticing it, live your way into the answer."

- Letter from RMR to Franz Xaver Kappus, 16 July 1903[94]
-

"Whoever lacks faith, lacks strength."

- Rainer Maria Rilke, The Florence Diary, 17 May 1898[95]

Unknown Artist, "May Calendar, Falconer Riding a Horse"
Leaf from a Book of Hours (Lille, France 13th century)

CALENDAR

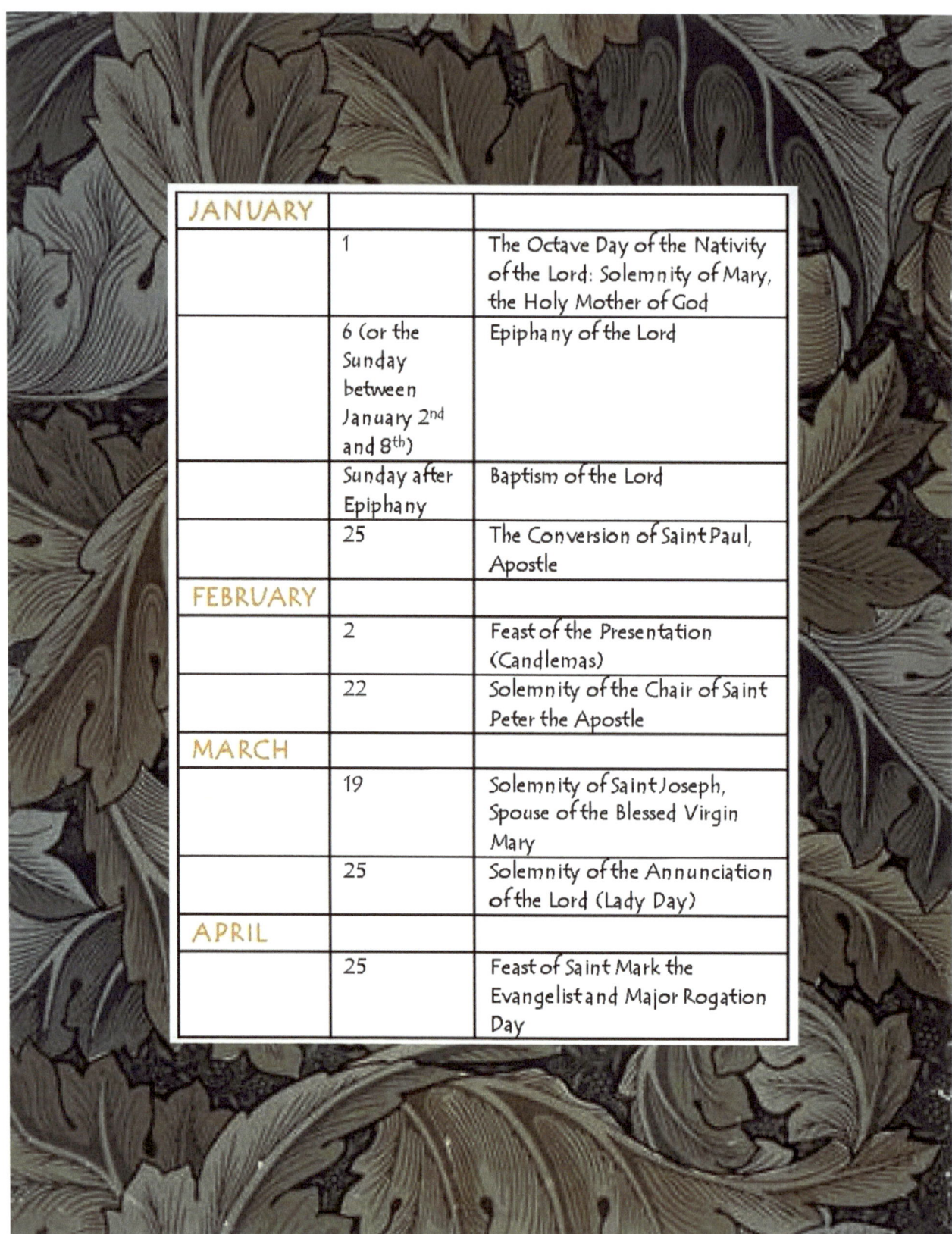

JANUARY		
	1	The Octave Day of the Nativity of the Lord: Solemnity of Mary, the Holy Mother of God
	6 (or the Sunday between January 2nd and 8th)	Epiphany of the Lord
	Sunday after Epiphany	Baptism of the Lord
	25	The Conversion of Saint Paul, Apostle
FEBRUARY		
	2	Feast of the Presentation (Candlemas)
	22	Solemnity of the Chair of Saint Peter the Apostle
MARCH		
	19	Solemnity of Saint Joseph, Spouse of the Blessed Virgin Mary
	25	Solemnity of the Annunciation of the Lord (Lady Day)
APRIL		
	25	Feast of Saint Mark the Evangelist and Major Rogation Day

William Morris, "Acanthus"

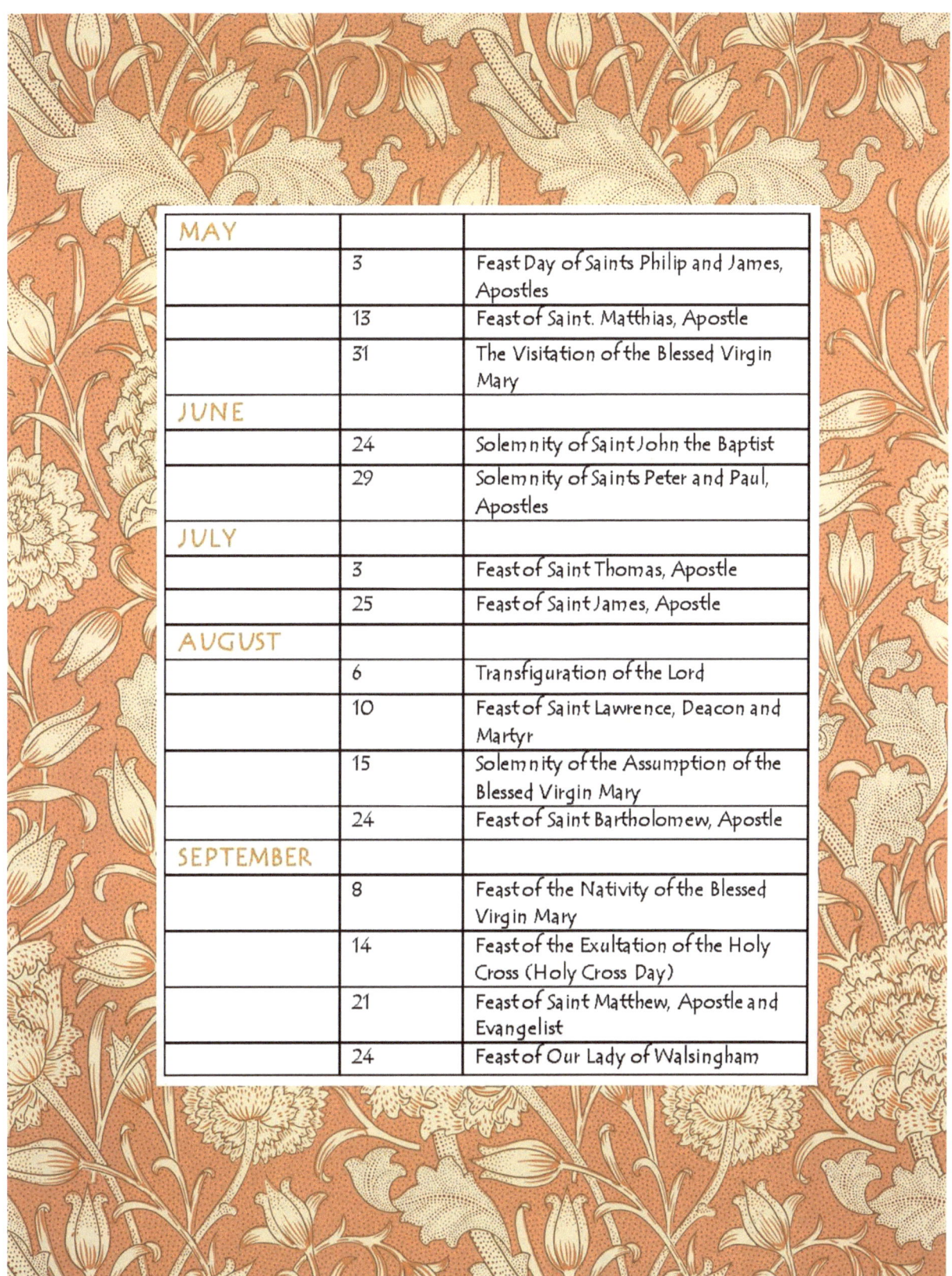

MAY		
	3	Feast Day of Saints Philip and James, Apostles
	13	Feast of Saint. Matthias, Apostle
	31	The Visitation of the Blessed Virgin Mary
JUNE		
	24	Solemnity of Saint John the Baptist
	29	Solemnity of Saints Peter and Paul, Apostles
JULY		
	3	Feast of Saint Thomas, Apostle
	25	Feast of Saint James, Apostle
AUGUST		
	6	Transfiguration of the Lord
	10	Feast of Saint Lawrence, Deacon and Martyr
	15	Solemnity of the Assumption of the Blessed Virgin Mary
	24	Feast of Saint Bartholomew, Apostle
SEPTEMBER		
	8	Feast of the Nativity of the Blessed Virgin Mary
	14	Feast of the Exultation of the Holy Cross (Holy Cross Day)
	21	Feast of Saint Matthew, Apostle and Evangelist
	24	Feast of Our Lady of Walsingham

William Morris, "Wild Tulips"

OCTOBER		
	4	Feast of Saint Francis
	18	Feast of Saint Luke, Apostle and Evangelist
	28	Feast of Saints Simon and Jude, Apostles
NOVEMBER		
	1	Solemnity of All Saints
	2	Commemoration of all the Faithful Departed (All Souls)
	9	Feast of the Dedication of the Lateran Basilica
	30	Feast of Saint Andrew, Apostle
	Last Sunday of the Church Year	Solemnity of our Lord Jesus Christ, King of the Universe
DECEMBER		
	8	Solemnity of the Immaculate Conception of the Virgin Mary
	12	Feast of Our Lady of Guadalupe
	25	The Nativity of the Lord (Christmas)
	26	Feast of Saint Stephen, the First Martyr
	27	Feast of Saint John, Apostle and Evangelist
	28	Feast of Holy Innocents, Martyrs
	Sunday within the Octave of Christmas or if no Sunday, December 30	Feast of the Holy Family of Jesus, Mary and Joseph

William Morris, "Willow Bough"

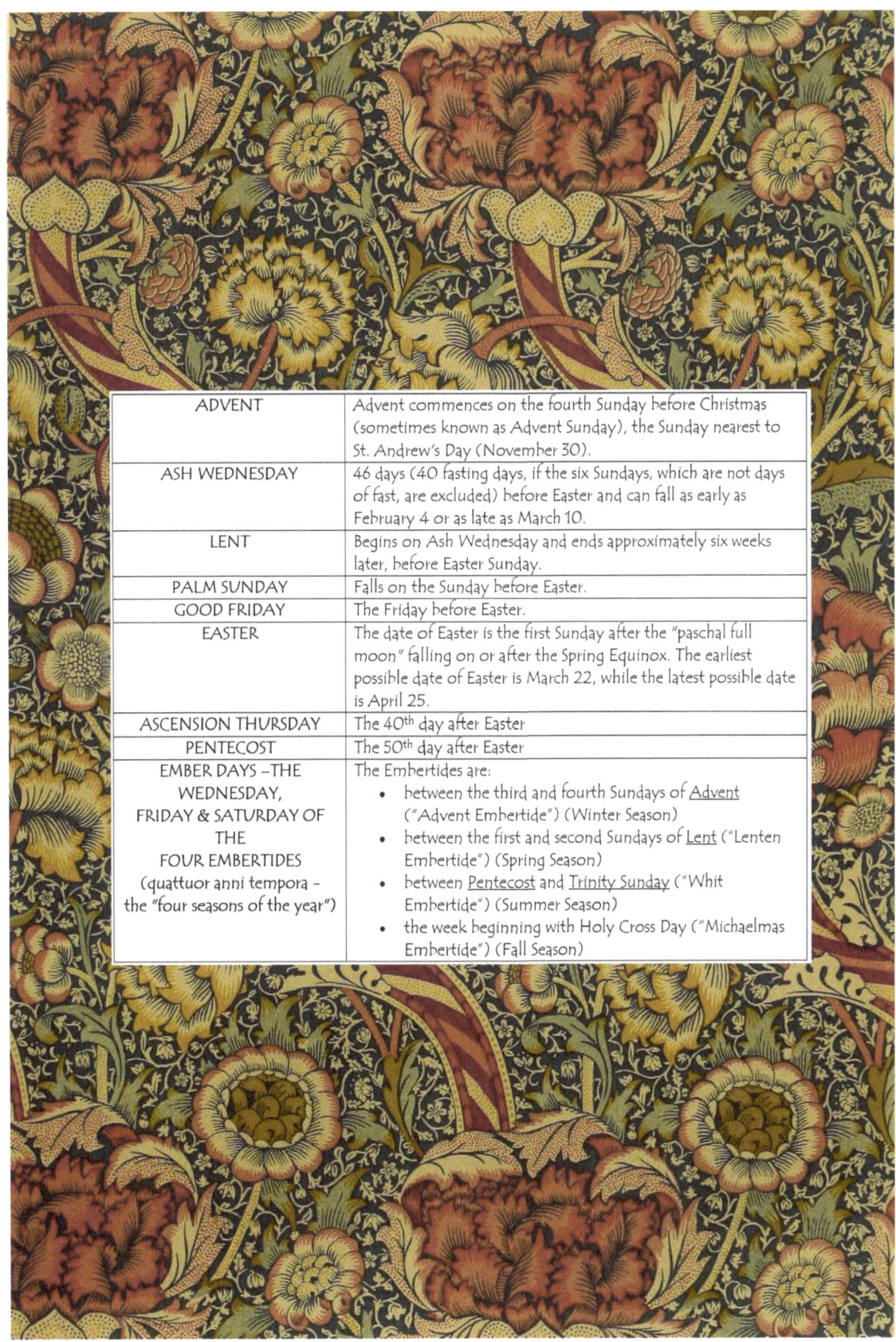

ADVENT	Advent commences on the fourth Sunday before Christmas (sometimes known as Advent Sunday), the Sunday nearest to St. Andrew's Day (November 30).
ASH WEDNESDAY	46 days (40 fasting days, if the six Sundays, which are not days of fast, are excluded) before Easter and can fall as early as February 4 or as late as March 10.
LENT	Begins on Ash Wednesday and ends approximately six weeks later, before Easter Sunday.
PALM SUNDAY	Falls on the Sunday before Easter.
GOOD FRIDAY	The Friday before Easter.
EASTER	The date of Easter is the first Sunday after the "paschal full moon" falling on or after the Spring Equinox. The earliest possible date of Easter is March 22, while the latest possible date is April 25.
ASCENSION THURSDAY	The 40th day after Easter
PENTECOST	The 50th day after Easter
EMBER DAYS – THE WEDNESDAY, FRIDAY & SATURDAY OF THE FOUR EMBERTIDES (quattuor anni tempora – the "four seasons of the year")	The Embertides are: • between the third and fourth Sundays of Advent ("Advent Embertide") (Winter Season) • between the first and second Sundays of Lent ("Lenten Embertide") (Spring Season) • between Pentecost and Trinity Sunday ("Whit Embertide") (Summer Season) • the week beginning with Holy Cross Day ("Michaelmas Embertide") (Fall Season)

William Morris, "Wandle"

Master of Walters, Leaf from the Barbavara Book of Hours
(Milan, Italy 15th century)

SEQUENCES OF THE GOSPELS

Matthäus Günther, "Saint Luke the Evangelist [Patron Saint of Artists] Painting the Virgin Mary"

My shadow, like a bowl, covers this day's work. And whether I paint or pray, it is Sunday, and I am like leaves and clay – an exultant Jerusalem in the valley. I am God's proud city, praising him in a hundred tongues; in me are David's psalms imbued, lying in the harp's twilight and breathing in the evening star. Upon rising, I walk my streets, long forsaken by my people, but it has made me more – I hear each walking in me, and expand my isolation from beginning to beginning.	So ist mein Tagwerk, über dem mein Schatten liegt wie eine Schale. Und bin ich auch wie Laub und Lehm, sooft ich bete oder male, ist Sonntag, und ich bin im Tale ein jubelndes Jerusalem. Ich bin die stolze Stadt des Herrn und sage ihn mit hundert Zungen; in mir ist Davids Dank verklungen: ich lag in Harfendämmerungen und atmete den Abendstern. Nach Aufgang gehen meine Gassen. Und ich bin lang vom Volk verlassen, so ist's: damit ich grösser bin. Ich höre jeden in mir schreiten und breite meine Einsamkeiten von Anbeginn zu Anbeginn.

"In the sixth month the angel Gabriel was sent from God to a city of Galilee named Nazareth, to a virgin betrothed to a man whose name was Joseph, of the house of David; and the virgin's name was Mary. And he came to her and said, 'Hail, full of grace, the Lord is with you!' But she was greatly troubled at the saying, and considered in her mind what sort of greeting this might be. And the angel said to her, 'Do not be afraid, Mary, for you have found favor with God. And behold, you will conceive in your womb and bear a son, and you shall call his name Jesus.'"

- Luke 1:26-31

Paolo Veneziano, "St. John the Baptist (fragment)"

"…in the high-priesthood of Annas and Cai'aphas, the word of God came to John the son of Zechari'ah in the wilderness; and he went into all the region about the Jordan, preaching a baptism of repentance for the forgiveness of sins. As it is written in the book of the words of Isaiah the prophet,

'The voice of one crying in the wilderness:
Prepare the way of the Lord,
make his paths straight.
Every valley shall be filled,
and every mountain and hill shall be brought low,
and the crooked shall be made straight,
and the rough ways shall be made smooth;
and all flesh shall see the salvation of God.'"

– Luke 3:2-6

I am alone in the world, but not alone enough, each Hour to worship. I am humble in the world, but not small enough, to be like an object before you, dark and wise. My will is my companion on the path to action; If someone unknowing nears in these quiet, expectant days, I would rather be alone. May I mirror you in all your forms and never be too blind or too old to hold up your heavy, ever-changing image. May I unfold and nowhere stay bent, for when bending, I lie. My mind must be true before you. I want to describe myself like a picture I saw, long and close, as a word understood, like my cup in my hand, like my mother's face, as a ship that carries me through the deadliest storm.	Ich bin auf der Welt zu allein und doch nicht allein genug, um jede Stunde zu weihn. Ich bin auf der Welt zu gering und doch nicht klein genug, um vor dir zu sein wie ein Ding, dunkel und klug. Ich will meinen Willen und will meinen Willen begleiten die Wege zur Tat; und will in stillen, irgendwie zögernden Zeiten, wenn etwas naht, unter den Wissenden sein oder allein. Ich will dich immer spiegeln in ganzer Gestalt, und will niemals blind sein oder zu alt um dein schweres schwankendes Bild zu halten. Ich will mich entfalten. Nirgends will ich gebogen bleiben, denn dort bin ich gelogen, wo ich gebogen bin. Und ich will meinen Sinn wahr vor dir. Ich will mich beschreiben wie ein Bild das ich sah, lange und nah, wie ein Wort, das ich begriff, wie meinen täglichen Krug, wie meiner Mutter Gesicht, wie ein Schiff, das mich trug durch den tödlichsten Sturm.

Ernst Barlach, "Reading Monks III"

"While the people pressed upon him to hear the word of God, he was standing by the lake of Gennes'aret. And he saw two boats by the lake; but the fishermen had gone out of them and were washing their nets. Getting into one of the boats, which was Simon's, he asked him to put out a little from the land. And he sat down and taught the people from the boat. And when he had ceased speaking, he said to Simon, 'Put out into the deep and let down your nets for a catch.' And Simon answered, 'Master, we toiled all night and took nothing! But at your word I will let down the nets.' And when they had done this, they enclosed a great shoal of fish; and as their nets were breaking, they beckoned to their partners in the other boat to come and help them… And Jesus said to Simon, 'Do not be afraid; henceforth you will be catching men.' And when they had brought their boats to land, they left everything and followed him."

- Luke 5:1–11

To the young Brother

This is taught –
leave confusion behind
and pray, as he did.
Be like those holy figures;
gilded in Church-golden tones,
holding sword and dignity on high.

And when you pray, say this:
    Trust me, my inner self,
I will not fail you;
I know that I am born of longing,
so many voices in my blood.

Alone with my feeling –
you much like a young girl,
cool and serious at first.
You overshadow my life.

There was a local woman once,
who waved in faded robes to me.
I heeded your call instead;
power beckoned me
from distant lands,
far beyond the hill's rim.

An den jungen Bruder

Dann bete du, wie es dich dieser lehrt,
der selber aus der Wirrnis wiederkehrt
und so, dass er zu heiligen Gestalten,
die alle ihres Wesens Würde halten,
in einer Kirche und auf goldnen Smalten
die Schönheit malte, und sie hielt ein Schwert.

Er lehrt dich sagen:
    Du mein tiefer Sinn,
vertraue mir, dass ich dich nicht enttäusche;
in meinem Blute sind so viel Geräusche,
ich aber weiss, dass ich aus Sehnsucht bin.

Ein grosser Ernst bricht über mich herein.
In seinem Schatten ist das Leben kühl.
Ich bin zum erstenmal mit dir allein,
du, mein Gefühl.
Du bist so mädchenhaft.

Es war ein Weib in meiner Nachbarschaft
und winkte mir aus welkenden Gewändern.
Du aber sprichst mir von so fernen Ländern.
Und meine Kraft
schaut nach den Hügelrändern.

Claude Monet, "Rouen Cathedral, West Façade, Sunlight"

Workers are we: apprentice, journeyman, master – all building you, high middle nave. And sometimes a learned traveler, excited, shows us a new approach, it flashes fast as light through our hundred spirits. We climb the overarching scaffolds, hammers hanging heavy in our hands, until the first hour's light, her radiant kiss on our foreheads, knowing that like the wind from the sea, all comes from you. Then the clangs of many hammers, pierces the mountains stroke for stroke; only twilight silences our work as your shape dawns. God, you are great.	**W**erkleute sind wir: Knappen, Jünger, Meister, und bauen dich, du hohes Mittelschiff. Und manchmal kommt ein ernster Hergereister, geht wie ein Glanz durch unsere hundert Geister und zeigt uns zitternd einen neuen Griff. Wir steigen in die wiegenden Gerüste, in unsern Händen hängt der Hammer schwer, bis eine Stunde uns die Stirnen küsste, die strahlend und als ob sie Alles wüsste von dir kommt wie der Wind vom Meer. Dann ist ein Hallen von dem vielen Hämmern, und durch die Berge geht es Stoss um Stoss. Erst wenn es dunkelt, lassen wir dich los: Und deine kommenden Konturen dämmern. Gott, du bist gross.

"And he said to his disciples, 'Therefore I tell you, do not be anxious about your life, what you shall eat, nor about your body, what you shall put on. For life is more than food, and the body more than clothing. Consider the ravens: they neither sow nor reap, they have neither storehouse nor barn, and yet God feeds them… Consider the lilies, how they grow; they neither toil nor spin; yet I tell you, even Solomon in all his glory was not clothed like one of these. But if God so clothes the grass which is alive in the field today and tomorrow is thrown into the oven, how much more will he clothe you, O men of little faith!'"

- Luke 12:22-28

"… This last week I was in the Bibliotheque Nationale from 10:00 AM to 5:00 PM every day and read many books and saw many reproductions of cathedrals from the twelfth and thirteenth centuries…that was great, great art. The more one examines its creations, the more deeply one can appreciate the value and magnificence of the work; for these cathedrals, these mountains and mountain ranges of the Middle Ages, would never have been finished if they had had to depend solely on inspiration for their creation. Hand had to be applied to work day after day, and if each day wasn't an inspiration, still each was a path to it."

- Letter from RMR to Clara Rilke, 16 September 1902[96]

Arnold Böcklin, "Spring in a Narrow Gorge"

Because the One sought you once, I know that you are open to us. But what if we scorn your depths? When a mountain has gold that no one seeks to mine, the river carries it forth to the day, and reveals it once in veined fullness, in the silence of the stones. Even when we do not wish it, *God ripens.*	Daraus, dass Einer dich einmal gewollt hat, weiss ich, dass wir dich wollen dürfen. Wenn wir auch alle Tiefen verwürfen: wenn ein Gebirge Gold hat und keiner mehr es ergraben mag, trägt es einmal der Fluss zutag, der in die Stille der Steine greift, der vollen. Auch wenn wir nicht wollen: *Gott reift.*

"And when a great crowd came together and people from town after town came to him, he said in a parable: 'A sower went out to sow his seed; and as he sowed, some fell along the path, and was trodden under foot, and the birds of the air devoured it. And some fell on the rock; and as it grew up, it withered away, because it had no moisture. And some fell among thorns; and the thorns grew with it and choked it. And some fell into good soil and grew, and yielded a hundredfold.' As he said this, he called out, 'He who has ears to hear, let him hear.'

And when his disciples asked him what this parable meant, he said, 'To you it has been given to know the secrets of the kingdom of God; but for others they are in parables, so that seeing they may not see, and hearing they may not understand. Now the parable is this: The seed is the word of God. The ones along the path are those who have heard; then the devil comes and takes away the word from their hearts, that they may not believe and be saved. And the ones on the rock are those who, when they hear the word, receive it with joy; but these have no root, they believe for a while and in time of temptation fall away. And as for what fell among the thorns, they are those who hear, but as they go on their way they are choked by the cares and riches and pleasures of life, and their fruit does not mature. And as for that in the good soil, they are those who, hearing the word, hold it fast in an honest and good heart, and bring forth fruit with patience.'"

- Luke 8:4-15

Zanobi di Benedetto Strozzi, "The Virgin Mary",
Leaf from the Adimari Book of Hours (Florence, Italy 15th century)

HOURS OF THE VIRGIN, THE CROSS AND THE HOLY SPIRIT

MATINS & LAUDS

(Midnight to early morning, ending at sunrise)

Lawrence Saint, painting of a panel from the "Acts of Mercy" stained glass window in All Saints' Church, York, England

God, my neighbor –
I know you are alone close by,
though I seldom hear you breathe.
So sometimes in the long night,
I disturb you
with hard raps on the wall;
for in your groping need, there is no one
to hand you a drink.
I listen always – give me a sign.
I am very near.

Perchance what separates us
is just a narrow wall –
it could be broken down,
totally without noise or sound,
with just one call from your mouth
or from mine.

It is built up from your icons.

And your portraits, like names, obscure you.
Their light flares and burns my
inner depth that knows you,
just to brighten their frames.

And my senses, which quickly fade,
are homeless and separated from you.

Du, Nachbar Gott, wenn ich dich manches Mal
in langer Nacht mit hartem Klopfen störe –
so ists, weil ich dich selten atmen höre
und weiss: Du bist allein im Saal.
Und wenn du etwas brauchst, ist keiner da,
um deinem Tasten einen Trank zu reichen:
Ich horche immer. Gib ein kleines Zeichen.
Ich bin ganz nah.

Nur eine schmale Wand ist zwischen uns,
durch Zufall; denn es könnte sein:
ein Rufen deines oder meines Munds –
und sie bricht ein
ganz ohne Lärm und Laut.

Aus deinen Bildern ist sie aufgebaut.

Und deine Bilder stehn vor dir wie Namen.
Und wenn einmal das Licht in mir entbrennt,
mit welchem meine Tiefe dich erkennt,
vergeudet sichs als Glanz auf ihren Rahmen.

Und meine Sinne, welche schnell erlahmen,
sind ohne Heimat und von dir getrennt.

Ernst Barlach, "Hovering Angel"

I live my life in widening rings, each covering more of below. I may not make it to the last, but I will try. I circle around God, around that ancient tower, in thousand-year orbits. And I still know not: am I falcon, or storm or a great song.	Ich lebe mein Leben in wachsenden Ringen, die sich über die Dinge ziehn. Ich werde den letzten vielleicht nicht vollbringen, aber versuchen will ich ihn. Ich kreise um Gott, um den uralten Turm, und ich kreise jahrtausendelang; und ich weiss noch nicht: bin ich ein Falke, ein Sturm oder ein grosser Gesang.

"Greatest of all are those star-filled nights, blossoming moonless in the dark and sowing shooting stars in abundance; some that fall quickly, suddenly and unexpectedly going out as if falling into water; flaming ones that jump from one star into another, as if they had measured their leap; and quiet ones that fly like birds with outstretched wings in a flat arc crosswise through the sky, materializing between two stars and disappearing between two others, as if the sky were only a passageway for them – not a place for them to stay."

- Letter from RMR to Clara Rilke, 8 April 1907[97]

Auguste Rodin, "The Hand of God"

I parse it from your Word, from the story of your gestures in the act of Making, your hands warm and wise, rounding and shaping. you said *live* our loud and *die* softly and over and over: *be* but before the first death came a murder – a tear in your flawless circle – a cry that tore away the voices, which 'til then had sung in unison, their praises your chariot and a bridge over the abyss. But since that time what they stammer are just shards of your ancient name.	Ich lese es heraus aus deinem Wort, aus der Geschichte der Gebärden, mit welchen deine Hände um das Werden sich ründeten, begrenzend, warm und weise. Du sagtest leben laut und sterben leise und wiederholtest immer wieder: Sein. Doch vor dem ersten Tode kam der Mord. Da ging ein Riss durch deine reifen Kreise und ging ein Schrein und riss die Stimmen fort, die eben erst sich sammelten um dich zu sagen, um dich zu tragen, alles Abgrunds Brücke – Und was sie seither stammelten, sind Stücke deines alten Namens.

Odilon Redon, "Cain and Abel"

Pale Abel speaks:

I am no more.
I saw not
what my brother did
when his face came between
the light and my face.
He is now alone,
but still alive, I think.
For who would do to him,
what he did to me.
All who walk my path
meet his anger
and are lost to him.

My older brother, I think,
Is a watchful judge;
but the Night thinks of me,
not him.

Der blasse Abelknabe spricht:

Ich bin nicht. Der Bruder hat mir was getan,
was meine Augen nicht sahn.
Er hat mir das Licht verhängt.
Er hat mein Gesicht verdrängt
mit seinem Gesicht.
Er ist jetzt allein.
Ich denke, er muss noch sein.
Denn ihm tut niemand, wie er mir getan.
Es gingen alle meine Bahn,
kommen alle vor seinen Zorn,
gehen alle an ihm verlorn.

Ich glaube, mein grosser Bruder wacht
wie ein Gericht.
An mich hat die Nacht gedacht;
an ihn nicht.

Emil Orlik, "Figure Under Willow Tree"

I love the dark hours of my being in which my senses immerse; in them I find, as in old letters, my daily life already lived remembered like legends, distant victories. From them, I know I have room for a second life, wide and timeless. Like a rich, ripe tree, I sometimes shelter the departed youth's grave, my roots embracing him, his dream once lost in song and sorrow, fulfilled.	Ich liebe meines Wesens Dunkelstunden, in welchen meine Sinne sich vertiefen; in ihnen hab ich, wie in alten Briefen, mein täglich Leben schon gelebt gefunden und wie Legende weit und überwunden. Aus ihnen kommt mir Wissen, dass ich Raum zu einem zweiten zeitlos breiten Leben habe. Und manchmal bin ich wie der Baum, der, reif und rauschend, über einem Grabe den Traum erfüllt, den der vergangne Knabe (um den sich seine warmen Wurzeln drängen) verlor in Traurigkeiten und Gesängen.

Ernst Barlach, "The First Day"

Your first word was: *Light* –
and all of time unfolded.
After a long, quiet hesitation,
with mindful countenance
and darkening tone we fear still,
came your second word: Man.

I do not wish to hear your third.

Oft I pray to you at night:
be rather the silent one,
inspire our spirits in dreams,
inscribe on our foreheads
and on mountains
the heavy sum of silence,
which grows in gestures.

Expelled from paradise at night –
wrath followed the unspeakable.
Be a refuge – our guardian
with a horn, but let one
just say, that the horn sounded.

Dein allererstes Wort war: Licht:
da ward die Zeit. Dann schwiegst du lange.
Dein zweites Wort ward Mensch und bange
(wir dunkeln noch in seinem Klange),
und wieder sinnt dein Angesicht.

Ich aber will dein drittes nicht.

Ich bete nachts oft: Sei der Stumme,
der wachsend in Gebärden bleibt
und den der Geist im Traume treibt,
dass er des Schweigens schwere Summe
in Stirnen und Gebirge schreibt.

Sei du die Zuflucht vor dem Zorne,
der das Unsagbare verstiess.
Es wurde Nacht im Paradies:
sei du der Hüter mit dem Horne,
und man erzählt nur, dass er blies.

Auguste Rodin, "Eternal Spring"

God speaks each of us alone, before he makes us and walks silently with us out of the night. but the clouded words at each beginning are the same: *Expand your senses to the limits of your longing: be my raiment.* *Become the fire behind, so that your shadow, stretched, always is upon me.* *Let everything happen to you – beauty and horror. One must only go forward: no feeling is too far. Do not let yourself be separated from me. The world is nearby, that they call life* *You will know it, because it is serious.* *Give me your hand.*	Gott spricht zu jedem nur, eh er ihn macht, dann geht er schweigend mit ihm aus der Nacht. Aber die Worte, eh jeder beginnt, diese wolkigen Worte, sind: Von deinen Sinnen hinausgesandt, geh bis an deiner Sehnsucht Rand; gib mir Gewand. Hinter den Dingen wachse als Brand, dass ihre Schatten, ausgespannt, immer mich ganz bedecken. Lass dir Alles geschehn: Schönheit und Schrecken. Man muss nur gehn: kein Gefühl ist das fernste. Lass dich von mir nicht trennen. Nah ist das Land, das sie das Leben nennen. Du wirst es erkennen an seinem Ernste. Gib mir die Hand.

"We have no reason to mistrust our world, for it is not against us. If it has horrors, they are our horrors; if it has chasms, these chasms belong to us; if dangers are there, we must try to love them. And if only we direct our life in accordance with the precept which advises us to rely always on what is difficult, then what appears to us now as the most alien will become our truest and most trusted experience. How could we forget those old myths that stand at the origin of all peoples – the myths about dragons that at the very last moment are changed into princesses? Perhaps all the dragons of our lives are really princesses who are waiting only to see us act, just once, with beauty and courage."

- Letter from RMR to Franz Xaver Kappus, 12 August 1904[98]

Lorado Taft, "Solitude of the Soul"

Just once, if total silence could find me
awake, but set free from the static of my senses,
from the laughter nearby
and all that is accidental and inexact –

At that moment,
in a thousand-fold thought
I might be transported to your outer limit –
hold on to you, if only for the length of a smile,
in order to return and gift you
to all of life, as thanks.

Wenn es nur einmal so ganz stille wäre.
Wenn das Zufällige und Ungefähre
verstummte und das nachbarliche Lachen,
wenn das Geräusch, das meine Sinne machen,
mich nicht so sehr verhinderte am Wachen –

Dann könnte ich in einem tausendfachen
Gedanken bis an deinen Rand dich denken
und dich besitzen (nur ein Lächeln lang),
um dich an alles Leben zu verschenken
wie einen Dank.

PRIME

(First hour after dawn, around 6:00 A.M.)

Heinrich Vogeler, "The Virgin Mary"

There was one beloved,
a haunted maid of shy and startling beauty,
in her were a hundred paths,
undiscovered and blooming,
awakened to fruition.

Let go, as if hovering, freed from gravity
in the Spring of her youth –
Her life, a wonder in royal service,
chimed in festive peals through all;
and she, once girlishly scattered,
now appeared to shine, enough for thousands;
so fulfilled in her heart – a vineyard for the One.

Da ward auch die zur Frucht Erweckte,
die schüchterne und schönerschreckte,
die heimgesuchte Magd geliebt.
Die Blühende, die Unentdeckte,
in der es hundert Wege gibt.

Da liessen sie gehn und schweben
und treiben mit dem jungen Jahr;
ihr dienendes Marien-Leben
ward königlich und wunderbar.
Wie feiertägliches Geläute
ging es durch alle Häuser gross;
und die einst mädchenhaft Zerstreute
war so versenkt in ihren Schoss
und so erfüllt von jenem Einen
und so für Tausende genug,
dass alles schien, sie zu bescheinen,
die wie ein Weinberg war und trug.

Auguste Rodin, "John the Baptist"

The poets have scattered you (a storm, their stammering) I would rather gather you again into the vessel that delights you. A wanderer in many winds that you drive thousand-fold, I gather all of you I find: a cup needed by the blind, the servants hid you deep, but the beggar held you out; and sometimes within a child, was a great fragment of your mind. You see, I am a seeker. One who needs the shepherd to turn away the stranger's gaze, deceiving - my face hidden from him. One who dreams of your completion, that will complete himself as well.	Die Dichter haben dich verstreut (es ging ein Sturm durch alles Stammeln), ich aber will dich wieder sammeln in dem Gefäss, dass dich erfreut. Ich wanderte in vielem Winde; da triebst du tausendmal darin. Ich bringe alles, was ich finde: als Becher brauchte dich der Blinde, sehr tief verbarg dich das Gesinde, der Bettler aber hielt dich hin; und manchmal war bei einem Kinde ein grosses Stück von deinem Sinn. Du siehst, dass ich ein Sucher bin. Einer, der hinter seinen Händen verborgen geht und wie ein Hirt; (mögst du den Blick, der ihn beirrt, den Blick der Fremden von ihm wenden). Einer, der träumt, dich zu vollenden und: dass er sich vollenden wird.

"...*John* comes to life with the eloquent, agitated arms, with the great stride of one who feels that Another will follow him. The body of this man is not untested: the desert wastes have scorched him through, hunger has tortured him, thirst of every kind has tested him. He has come through all and has become hardened. The gaunt, ascetic body is like a wooden handle in which his stride's wide fork is set. He goes. He advances as though all the world's distances were within him, as if he were measuring them with his stride. He goes. His arms express his movement, his fingers spead and seem to make the sign of striding in the air." –Rainer Maria Rilke, Monograph on Auguste Rodin[99]

Ernst Barlach, "The Ascetic"

You see, I want much.
Perhaps I want everything:
the darkness of each unending fall
and every glittering playful climb.

So many live who wish for nothing,
ruled by flat feelings
from their soft judgments.

But you rejoice at the faces
of those who serve in thirst.

Those who need you
like a tool –
make you happy.

You still are not cold
and it is not too late
to dive into your depths,
expectant and quiet,
where life is revealed.

Du siehst, ich will viel.
Vielleicht will ich alles:
das Dunkel jedes unendlichen Falles
und jedes Steigens lichtzitterndes Spiel.

Es leben so viele und wollen nichts
und sind durch ihres leichten Gerichts
glatte Gefühle gefürstet.

Aber du freust dich jedes Gesichts,
das dient und dürstet.

Du freust dich aller, die dich gebrauchen
wie ein Gerät.

Noch bist du nicht kalt, und es ist nicht zu spät,
in deine werdenden Tiefen zu tauchen,
wo sich das Leben ruhig verrät.

Ivan Kramskoy, "Christ in the Wilderness"

"… Jesus came from Galilee to the Jordan to John, to be baptized by him … Then Jesus was led up by the Spirit into the wilderness to be tempted by the devil. And he fasted forty days and forty nights, and afterward he was hungry. And the tempter came and said to him, 'If you are the Son of God, command these stones to become loaves of bread.' But he answered, 'It is written, 'Man shall not live by bread alone, but by every word that proceeds from the mouth of God'' …

Then the devil left him, and behold, angels came and ministered to him."

- Matthew 3:13, 4:1-11

I am, you anxious one.

As my thoughts break against you,
do you not hear me?
As my winged senses circle,
white around your face
and my spirit stands before you
close in a mantle of silence,
do you not see me?
Does not my prayer
ripen before your eyes as on a tree in May?

When you sleep, I am what you dream
and when you wake, I am what you will —
for I will be there, mighty
in star-silent glory, encircling the city
in the strangeness of time.

Ich bin, du Ängstlicher. Hörst du mich nicht
mit allen meinen Sinnen an dir branden?
Meine Gefühle, welche Flügel fanden,
umkreisen weiss dein Angesicht.
Siehst du nicht meine Seele, wie sie dicht
vor dir in einem Kleid aus Stille steht?
Reift nicht mein mailiches Gebet
an deinem Blicke wie an einem Baum?

Wenn du der Träumer bist, bin ich dein Traum.
Doch wenn du wachen willst, bin ich dein Wille
und werde mächtig aller Herrlichkeit
und runde mich wie einer Sternenstille
über der wunderlichen Stadt der Zeit.

Frédéric Auguste Bartholdi, "Funerary Genius"

I cannot believe the small death we see daily overhead remains our worry and distress I cannot believe its threat is serious, I still live – have time to build; more red than roses is my blood. My mind is deeper than the game, in which Death laughingly delights. I am the world, from which he erring fell. You don't know if Death is the same, like monks circling round – Is it two, ten, thousands or more? One is afraid of their return. You see only the strange yellow hand that stretches out naked and near, there and there- as if coming from your own robe.	Ich kann nicht glauben, dass der kleine Tod, dem wir doch täglich übern Scheitel schauen, uns eine Sorge bleibt und eine Not. Ich kann nicht glauben, dass er ernsthaft droht; ich lebe noch, ich habe Zeit zu bauen: mein Blut ist länger als die Rosen rot. Mein Sinn ist tiefer als das witzige Spiel mit unsrer Furcht, darin er sich gefällt. Ich bin die Welt, aus der er irrend fiel. Wie er kreisende Mönche wandern so umher; man fürchtet sich vor ihrer Wiederkehr, man weiss nicht: ist es jedesmal derselbe, Sind's zwei, sind's zehn, sind's tausend oder mehr? Man kennt nur diese fremde gelbe Hand, die sich ausstreckt so nackt und nah – da: als käm sie aus dem eigenen Gewand.

Alexander Ivanov, "The Last Supper"

Now the hour strikes and moves me, / with a clear, metallic tone – / my senses shiver – I feel my power / and grasp the sculptured day. Nothing can become in full / until I see it, my vision ripe – / and all becoming stands in silence, / like a bride waiting to be called. Nothing is too small for me to love, / to greatly paint on a golden tableau / and hold on high, / not knowing / whose soul it will set free.	Da neigt sich die Stunde und rührt mich an / mit klarem, metallenem Schlag: / mir zittern die Sinne. Ich fühle: ich kann – / und ich fasse den plastischen Tag. Nichts war noch vollendet, eh ich es erschaut, / ein jedes Werden stand still. / Meine Blicke sind reif, und wie eine Braut / kommt jedem das Ding, das er will. Nichts ist mir zu klein und ich lieb es trotzdem / und mal' es auf Goldgrund und gross / und halte es hoch, und ich weiss nicht wem / löst es die Seele los…

Albrecht Dürer, "Christ on the Mount of Olives"

What will you do, God, when I die?
When I, your jug, lie broken?
When I, your drink, am spilt?
When I, your human cloak and craft—
your earthly sense – am gone?

Lost with me –
the home that greets you,
with words both close and warm
I am the velvet sandals
then dropped from your weary feet.

Your great robe,
fallen from your shoulders.
Your gaze, which touched my cheek,
warm as a kiss,
will come, will search for me, long,
only to find unfamiliar stones,
lifeless in the lap of sunset.

What will you do, God? I am troubled.

Was wirst du tun, Gott, wenn ich sterbe?
Ich bin dein Krug (wenn ich zerscherbe?)
Ich bin dein Trank (wenn ich verderbe?)
Bin dein Gewand und dein Gewerbe,
Mit mir verlierst du deinem Sinn.

Nach mir has du kein Haus, darin
dich Worte, nah und warm, begrüssen.
Es fällt von deinem müden Füssen
die Samtsandale, die ich bin.

Dein grosser Mantel lässt dich los.
Dein Blick, den ich mit meiner Wange
warm, wie mit einem Pfühl, empfange,
wird kommen, wird mich suchen, lange –
Und legt beim Sonnenuntergange
sich fremden Steinen in den Schoss.

Was wirst du tun, Gott? Ich bin bange.

TERCE

(The third hour, around 9:00 A.M.)

Édouard Manet, "The Head of Christ"

Like a guard in the wine lands,
keeping watch in his hut,
so am I, Lord, a hut in your hands,
and am night, O Lord, of your night.

Vineyard, pasture, old apple orchard,
field, that no Spring has overturned,
fig tree, that even in ground
as hard as marble, carries fruit
a hundred-fold:

Round branches waft juices' scent
and you ask not if I am watchful;
your depths flow silent past me,
all fear dissolved.

Wie der Wächter in den Weingeländen
seine Hütte hat und wacht,
bin ich Hütte, Herr, in deinen Händen
und bin Nacht, o Herr, von deiner Nacht.

Weinberg, Weide, alter Apfelgarten,
Acker, der kein Frühjahr überschlägt,
Feigenbaum, der auch im marmorharten
Grunde hundert Früchte trägt:

Duft geht aus deinen runden Zweigen.
Und du fragst nicht, ob ich wachsam sei;
furchtlos, aufgelöst in Säften, steigen
deine Tiefen still an mir vorbei.

SEXT

(The sixth hour, at mid-day)

Unknown Artist, "Crucifixion Icon" (Russia ca. 16th Century)

You see me as one pressed, at the precipice of this hour – but that is not my life. I am a tree in my landscape, just one voice among my many voices, that goes silent before its time.
 	
I make peace between two tones, as they are uneasy neighbors, for the knell of Death seeks to grow at their expense –
 	
But, trembling in that dark interval, they reconcile
     - and the song stays sweet.
	Mein Leben ist nicht diese steile Stunde, darin du mich so eilen siehst. Ich bin ein Baum vor meinem Hintergrunde, ich bin nur einer meiner vielen Munde und jener, welcher sich am frühsten schliesst.
	
	Ich bin die Ruhe zwischen zweien Tönen, die sich nur schlecht aneinander gewöhnen: denn der Ton Tod will sich erhöhn -
	
	Aber im dunklen Intervall versöhnen sich beide zitternd.
	    Und das Lied bleibt schön.

"...all these pieces, each in its own way, embody approximations of the border sensations of existence and all aspire towards that divinable balance I once found matchlessly represented in a fragment of ancient music. Romain Rolland, who played it for me, had found it in a Gregorian Mass. As I heard it and heard it again, I had the impression of two scale pans that, gently flattening out, came to rest opposite each other. I shared my impression with Rolland and only then did he confess to me that this was an ancient grave-stone inscription, an epitaph written with musical notes: the most striking validation of which certainly was that it could be grasped and understood through such a simile." –Letter from RMR to Countess Stauffenberg, 23 January 1919[100]

NONE

(The ninth hour, around 3 P.M.)

Albrecht Dürer, "Praying Hands"

In our time, from the poor city
to the distant place of unnamed paths,
none move their hands;
they lay quiet by their sides.
Speak out, daily blessing,
and say softly on a leaf:

in truth, prayer is all,
hands are sanctified for this,
and piety unfolds alike
from the hands of the painter
to the hands of the mower
and his grappling machine,
each work an entreaty.

We know that God,
like a great beard and cloak,
surrounds us in time,
ancient and eternal –
we sometimes hear it is manifold.
We are like veins in the basalt
of God's hard majesty.

Alle, die ihre Hände regen
nicht in der Zeit, der armen Stadt,
alle, die sie an Leises legen,
an eine Stelle, fern den Wegen,
die kaum noch einen Namen hat, –
sprechen dich aus, du Alltagssegen,
und sagen sanft auf einem Blatt:

Es gibt im Grunde nur Gebete,
so sind die Hände uns geweiht,
dass sie nichts schufen, was nicht flehte;
ob einer malte oder mähte,
schon aus dem Ringen der Geräte
entfaltete sich Frömmigkeit.

Die Zeit ist eine vielgestalte.
Wir hören manchmal von der Zeit,
und tun das Ewige und Alte;
wir wissen, dass uns Gott umwallte
gross wie ein Bart und wie ein Kleid.
Wir sind wie Adern im Basalte
in Gottes harter Herrlichkeit.

VESPERS

(Sunset)

Pierre-Étienne Monnot, "Virgin Mary Swooning Over the Dead Body of Christ at the Foot of the Cross"

But almost as if weighed down by the decay of the columns and arches- fruit-garlanded burden – and the passing of the Song, the Virgin senses the coming scars, in those different hours, as one still connected to the Greater. Her hands, silently loosened, lie empty. Woe - her greatest yet to bear. She is not comforted by angels in array around her - strange and terrible.	Aber als hätte die Last der Fruchtgehänge und der Verfall der Säulen und Bogengänge und der Abgesang der Gesänge sie beschwert, hat die Jungfrau sich in anderen Stunden, wie von Grösserem noch unentbunden, kommenden Wunden zugekehrt. Ihre Hände, die sich lautlos lösten, liegen leer. Wehe, sie gebar noch nicht den Grössten. Und die Engel, die nicht trösten, stehen fremd und furchtbar um sie her.

Vincent van Gogh,
"Pine Trees against a Red Sky with Setting Sun"

Light breaks through your treetops,	Es lärmt das Licht im Wipfel deines Baumes
and everything is made vainly colorful;	und macht dir alle Dinge bunt und eitel,
only when the day begins to dim	sie finden dich erst, wenn der Tag verglomm.
can they find you, a thousand hands	Die Dämmerung, die Zärtlichkeit des Raumes,
raised above a thousand heads –	legt tausend Hände über tausend Scheitel,
there, what is strange become pious.	und unter ihnen wird das Fremde fromm.
This is how you wish the world to hold you,	Du willst die Welt nicht anders an dich halten
just so, with the softest of gestures.	als so, mit dieser sanftesten Gebärde.
From the heavens you embrace the earth	Aus ihren Himmeln greifst du dir die Erde
and shelter it under the folds	und fühlst sie unter deines Mantels Falten.
of your mantel.	
	Du hast so eine leise Art zu sein.
You have such a quiet way,	Und jene, die dir laute Namen weihn,
that those who loudly	sind schon vergessen deiner Nachbarschaft.
give you holy names	
already are lost to you.	Von deinen Händen, die sich bergig heben,
	steigt, unsern Sinnen das Gesetz zu geben,
We rise to you,	mit dunkler Stirne deine stumme Kraft.
to the Law offered in your hands,	
hands that raised mountains	
with mute power	
and darkened brow.	

"…but there is one tree in the garden that also could stand in Tuscany, in an ancient cloister: a tall old cypress, overgrown with a train of wisteria, whose light blue-violet pendants fall and rise overall, even up to the top of the tree's darkness; – that is joy. That and the magnificent fig trees, standing there like Old Testament altar candlesticks with upcurving branches, slowly opening their light-green leaves."

- Letter from RMR to Lou Andreas-Salomé, 15 April 1904[101]

Unknown Artist, Detail of Leaf from an Antiphonary
[Book of Antiphons and Antiphonal Chants
Sung During the Canonical Hours]
(Venice, Italy, ca. 1505)

I love you, gentlest of laws, that gives us growth in return for struggle; you great home-yearning, that we cannot overcome; you forest, that engulfs us; you song we sing with silence, you dark net, in which our feelings are caught. So infinitely great have you become, since the day of our creation, you can come to rest now, realized in men, angels and Madonnas, planted so deep and broad and so richly overgrown under ages of your suns. Lay your hand on Heaven's rim and overlook, we pray, the darkness we do to you.	Ich liebe dich, du sanftestes Gesetz, an dem wir reiften, da wir mit ihm rangen; du grosses Heimweh, das wir nicht bezwangen, du Wald, aus dem wir nie hinausgegangen, du Lied, das wir mit jedem Schweigen sangen, du dunkles Netz, darin sich flüchtend die Gefühle fangen. Du hast dich so unendlich gross begonnen an jenem Tage, da du uns begannst, – und wir sind so gereift in deinen Sonnen, so breit geworden und so tief gepflanzt, dass du in Menschen, Engeln und Madonnen dich ruhend jetzt vollenden kannst. Lass deine Hand am Hang der Himmel ruhn und dulde stumm, was wir dir dunkel tun.

"Don't let the surfaces confuse you; in the depths all becomes law. And those who live the secret falsely and badly (and they are very many) lose it only for themselves and unknowingly pass it on like a sealed letter."

- Letter from RMR to Franz Xaver Kappus, 16 July 1903[102]

Jean-François Millet, "Shepherdess and Her Flock"

My soul,
it is an hour from the edge of day
and the land is prepared to hear you –
learn what you yearn for –
now say it:

Be heath, and heath, be wide.
Have ancient burial mounds,
barely recognizable, but growing
as the moonlight moves across
the long forgotten flat land.
Silence, arise and take shape.
Clothe all things – they are like children,
and are willingly embraced.
Be heath, be heath, be heath.

Then perhaps will come the old blind one,
as if conjoined with the night –
sitting, his thoughtful gaze unfocused,
home, heath and heaven
are all within his large dark world;
only the songs are lost to him.
My home listens in vain
for him to sound the first notes,
but time and the wind drank them
from the ears of thousands of fools.

Eine Stunde vom Rande des Tages,
und das Land ist zu allem bereit.
Was du sehnst, meine Seele, sag es:

Sei Heide und, Heide, sei weit.
Habe alte, alte Kurgane,
wachsend und kaum erkannt,
wenn es Mond wird über das plane
langvergangene Land.
Gestalte dich, Stille. Gestalte
die Dinge (es ist ihre Kindheit,
sie werden dir willig sein).
Sei Heide, sei Heide, sei Heide,
dann kommt vielleicht auch der Alte,
den ich kaum von der Nacht unterscheide,
und bringt seine riesige Blindheit
in mein horchendes Haus herein.

Ich seh ihn sitzen und sinnen,
nicht über mich hinaus;
für ihn ist alles innen,
Himmel und Heide und Haus.
Nur die Lieder sind ihm verloren,
die er nie mehr beginnt;
aus vielen tausend Ohren
trank sie die Zeit und der Wind;
aus den Ohren der Toren.

COMPLINE

(At bed-time)

Giuseppe Sanmartino (Circle of), "Veiled Christ"

I believe in the night –
you darkness that bore me.
I love you more than the flame
that confines this world
as it brightens it;
for as with any sphere,
you cannot know beyond it.

But the darkness embraces all,
takes all –
shapes and flames,
animals and me,
men and powers –

And I sense nearby,
a great force bestirs itself.

Du Dunkelheit, aus der ich stamme,
ich liebe dich mehr als die Flamme,
welche die Welt begrenzt,
indem sie glänzt
für irgendeinen Kreis,
aus dem heraus kein Wesen von ihr weiss.

Aber die Dunkelheit hält alles an sich:
Gestalten und Flammen, Tiere und mich,
wie sie's errafft,
Menschen und Mächte –

Und es kann sein: eine grosse Kraft
rührt sich in meiner Nachbarschaft.

Ich glaube an Nächte.

Unknown Artist, Ikon, "Christ's Descent into Hell" (Russia, 19th century)

"For Christ also died for sins once for all, the righteous for the unrighteous, that he might bring us to God, being put to death in the flesh but made alive in the spirit; in which he went and preached to the spirits in prison, who formerly did not obey, when God's patience waited in the days of Noah, during the building of the ark, in which a few, that is, eight persons, were saved through water."

- 1 Peter 3:18-20

As a pilgrim I entered,
forehead pressed against you,
torment-filled Stone.
With lights, seven in number
I surrounded your dark being
and saw in every image
your earthy birthmark.

Standing among the beggars,
drifting gaunt and ill,
I saw you, Wind, in the
pattern of their to and fro.

I saw a peasant,
old beyond measure
bearded like Joachim
and as his figure dimmed
in the press of those around,
you felt never so tender –
so without word revealed –
as in them and in him.

You let time run its course–
for you there is no rest therein.
The peasant finds your sense
picks it up and throws it hence
and picks it up again.

Da trat ich als ein Pilger ein
und fühlte voller Qual
an meiner Stirne dich, du Stein.
Mit Lichtern, sieben an der Zahl,
umstellte ich dein dunkles Sein
und sah in jedem Bilde dein
bräunliches Muttermal.

Da stand ich, wo die Bettler stehn,
die schlecht und hager sind:
aus ihrem Auf- und Niederwehn
begriff ich dich, du Wind.

Ich sah den Bauer, überjahrt,
bärtig wie Joachim,
und daraus, wie er dunkel ward,
von lauter Ähnlichen umschart,
empfand ich dich wie nie so zart,
so ohne Wort geoffenbart
in allen und in ihm.

Du lässt der Zeit den Lauf,
und dir ist niemals Ruh darin:
der Bauer findet deinen Sinn
und hebt ihn auf und wirft ihn hin
und hebt ihn wieder auf.

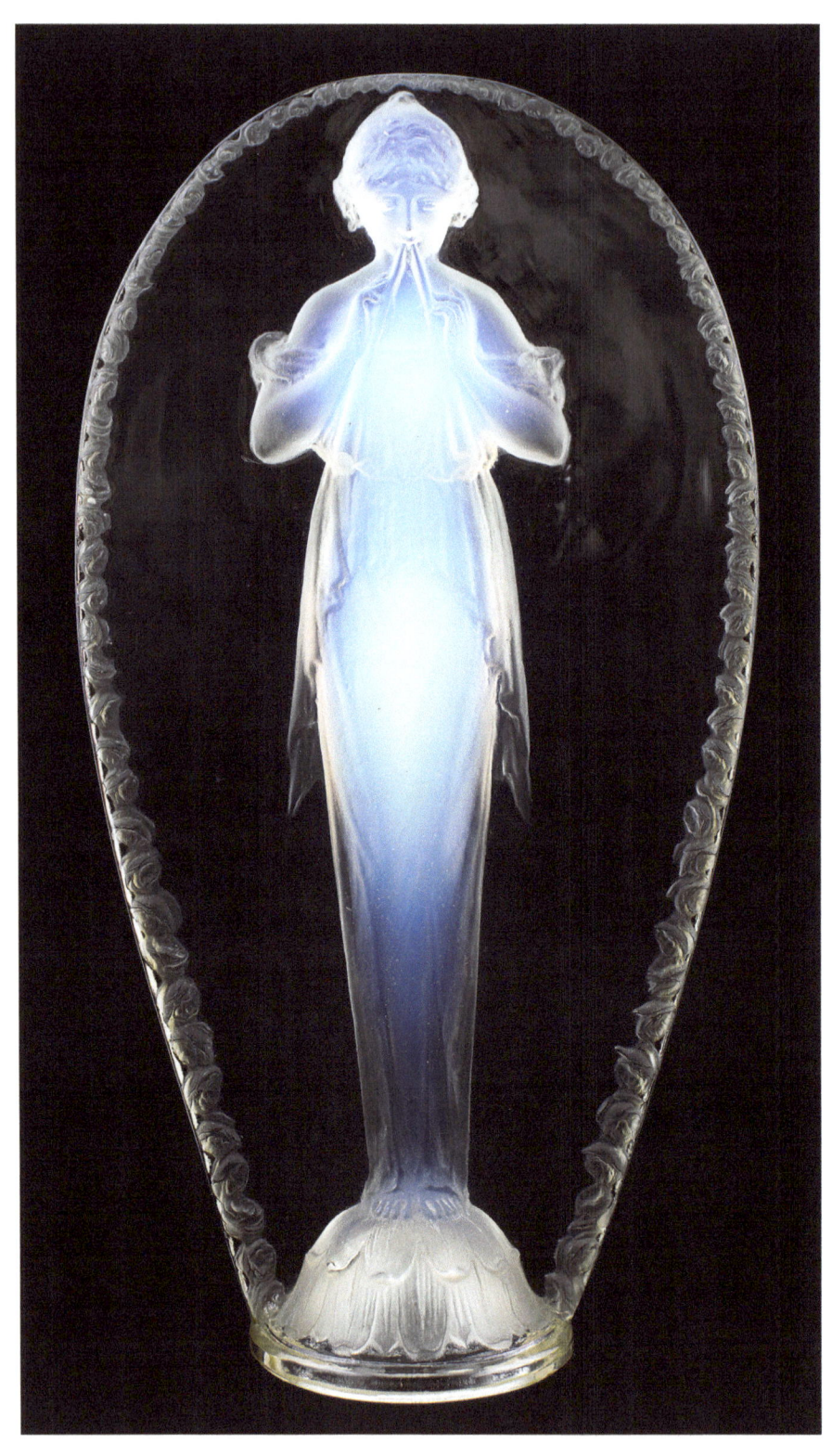

René Lalique, "Grande Ovale Joueuse de Flute"

Silent behind his beard, shaking, yearning for his lost melodies; it occurs to me that deep within me, I have saved each song for him. And as I kneel before him: the songs rush back to him.	Und dennoch: mir geschieht, als ob ich ein jedes Lied tief in mir ihm ersparte. Er schweigt hinterm bebenden Barte, er möchte sich wiedergewinnen aus seinen Melodien. Da komm ich zu seinen Knien: und seine Lieder rinnen rauschend zurück in ihn.

"… on the third day He rose again from the dead; He ascended into heaven, and is seated at the right hand of God the Father Almighty…" – excerpt from The Apostle's Creed

"…now we again have had a couple of days of bright sun and today it is raining, and over the wall across from me, a light wind is turning the leaves of the chestnut trees and acacias so that they are hit and feeling the rain from all sides and are glistening from it. And it is one of those rainy days that are not for the city. That one should experience outside the city, to see all the darkened green, the gray-mirrored meadows, the moving beech leaves, more varied in their green with the city lights no longer there (those bright, melting, dissolving lights), leaves that have only reflections - green seeing itself in green again, green set against green, with green shadows, green that has deepened so as finally to have a bottom somewhere, a foundation of green. And suddenly all the color is taken out of the scent, too, as if the setting sun had let it sink into the flowers. Now the leaves are fragrant, the little beech leaves above all, and the old-fashioned leaves of the elms and the little turned-over leaves of the balsam poplars are flowing slowly out into the air."

- Letter from RMR to Clara Rilke, 1 June 1906[103]

Unknown Artist, "Risen Christ" (Florence, Italy ca. 1620)

With a bough like no other, God, the tree, rustles richly, announcing Summer; in a land, where those listening are as solitary as I. Revelation comes just to the solitary and more will be given to those united, than if alone in their solitude. To each then another God appears, differenced hundred-fold, until, close to tears, they see through their mile-wide beliefs, their assents and denials – *one* God move like a wave, This is the last of all prayers, said to themselves by the knowing: *God's roots have borne fruit, go forth and ring the bells; the Hour is ripe as still days approach. God's roots have borne fruit, watch in earnest.*	Mit einem Ast, der jenem niemals glich, wird Gott, der Baum, auch einmal sommerlich verkündend werden und aus Reife rauschen; in einem Lande, wo die Menschen lauschen, wo jeder ähnlich einsam ist wie ich. Denn nur dem Einsamen wird offenbart, und vielen Einsamen der gleichen Art wird mehr gegeben als dem schmalen Einen. Denn jedem wird ein andrer Gott erscheinen, bis sie erkennen, nah am Weinen, dass durch ihr meilenweites Meinen, durch ihr Vernehmen und Verneinen, verschieden nur in hundert Seinen ein Gott wie eine Welle geht. Das ist das endlichste Gebet, das dann die Sehenden sich sagen: Die Wurzel Gott hat Frucht getragen, geht hin, die Glocken zu zerschlagen; wir kommen zu den stillern Tagen, in denen reif die Stunde steht. Die Wurzel Gott hat Frucht getragen. Seid ernst und seht.

"On the way to Pietra Santa there is a bleeding mountain. It pulls the olive trees away from its gray stone body like a dusty pilgrim's cloak and displays to the dreaming valley below, that did not wish to believe in it, the wound in its breast: red marble, ingrained in its graying torso."

- Rainer Maria Rilke, The Florence Diary, 22 May 1898[104]

"If God has given a law, then it is this: Be alone from time to time. For he can come only to a solitary one – or to a pair he can no longer tell apart."

- Rainer Maria Rilke, The Schmargendorf Diary, Night, 25 November 1899[105]

Unknown Artist, "The Dove (Holy Spirit) in Stained Glass"

"But he, full of the Holy Spirit, gazed into heaven and saw the glory of God…"
- Acts 7:55

You come and go, the doors closing much softer, air almost undisturbed. You are the most quiet of all who go through the homes. So accustomed are we to you, our eyes remain on the book, its pictures now illuminated and vibrant in resonance with you – at once soft and loud – from the blue of your shadow, Oft in my mind's eye, I see your image – like a kaleidoscope deer; your fragments move light but loudly in my dark forest. Then I am standing on your wheel, your many dark axles turning ever closer to me – one heavier than the others – and with every revolution, my willed creation grows.	Du kommst und gehst. Die Türen fallen viel sanfter zu, fast ohne Wehn. Du bist der Leiseste von allen, die durch die leisen Häuser gehn. Man kann sich so an dich gewöhnen, dass man nicht aus dem Buche schaut, wenn seine Bilder sich verschönen, von deinem Schatten überblaut; weil dich die Dinge immer tönen nur einmal leis und einmal laut. Oft wenn ich dich in Sinnen sehe, verteilt sich deine Allgestalt; du gehst wie lauter lichte Rehe, und ich bin dunkel und bin Wald. Du bist ein Rad, an dem ich stehe: von deinen vielen dunklen Achsen wird immer wieder eine schwer und dreht sich näher zu mir her, und meine willigen Werke wachsen von Wiederkehr zu Wiederkehr.

Lorenzo Ghiberti, Detail of Panel from the Gates of Paradise, Baptistery of San Giovanni, Florence, Italy

In your name, a thousand theologians immersed themselves in night, young maids awakened to you and shimmering youths rushed to you in silver battle. In your long archways, the poets met – mild, deep and masterful – kings of sounds. And in your gentle evening hours, you press darkly in the mouth affecting all poets alike; they sense the treasure and garb you in splendor To you are raised a hundred thousand harps – a swaying out of silence – and your old winds cast away all things and fears, the breath of your majesty.	Es tauchten tausend Theologen in deines Namens alte Nacht. Jungfrauen sind zu dir erwacht, und Jünglinge in Silber zogen und schimmerten in dir, du Schlacht. In deinen langen Bogengängen begegneten die Dichter sich und waren Könige von Klängen und mild und tief und meisterlich. Du bist die sanfte Abendstunde, die alle Dichter ähnlich macht; du drängst dich dunkel in die Munde, und im Gefühl von einem Funde umgibt ein jeder dich mit Pracht. Dich heben hunderttausend Harfen wie Schwingen aus der Schweigsamkeit. Und deine alten Winde warfen zu allen Dingen und Bedarfen den Hauch von deiner Herrlichkeit.

Master of Walters, Detail of Leaf
from the Barbavara Book of Hours (Milan, Italy 15th century)

Giovan Pietro Birago,
"Initial D with David in Prayer"

THE PENITENTIAL PSALMS AND PILGRIM PSALMS

Auguste Rodin, "The Storm"

"Now it is Fall where you are, and you are walking in the forest, in the great forest into which one already can see so far, into the wind that transforms the world...I think of evenings before the stormy night that strips everything withered from the trees, and think of the storm itself, of the night that flies past the stars into morning. Into the empty, new, clear, storm-swept morning...."

- Letter from RMR to Lou Andreas-Salomé, 3 November 1903[106]

112

Standing by the window,
the storm's fury does not awe you -
though the trees bend before it -
for your senses praise and seek
the one from whom they flee,
creating footpaths by their flight.

When you picked fruit
you believed you recognized the force,
that makes the trees' blood rise,
then fall again, you think,
as Summer's weeks come to rest -
an enigma - the source of all -
and again you are a guest.

Now comes the great solitude
as the days become numb;
you must leave your home of Summer,
taking your heart to the plains,
the world, like old leaves,
blown from your senses by the wind.

The sky is all you have;
be now earth, land and evening song
under its watchful gaze.
Be humble now, like a thing
poised to be real,
so He of the tidings
feels you in his grasp.

Dich wundert nicht des Sturmes Wucht, -
du hast ihn wachsen sehn; -
die Bäume flüchten. Ihre Flucht
schafft schreitende Alleen.
Da weisst du, der, vor dem sie fliehn,
ist der, zu dem du gehst,
und deine Sinne singen ihn,
wenn du am Fenster stehst.

Des Sommers Wochen standen still,
es stieg der Bäume Blut;
jetzt fühlst du, dass es fallen will
in den der alles tut.
Du glaubtest schon erkannt die Kraft,
als du die Frucht erfasst,
jetzt wird sie wieder rätselhaft,
und du bist wieder Gast.

Der Sommer war so wie dein Haus,
drin weisst du alles stehn -
jetzt musst du in dein Herz hinaus
wie in die Ebene gehn.
Die grosse Einsamkeit beginnt,
die Tage werden taub,
aus deinen Sinnen nimmt der Wind
die Welt wie welkes Laub.

Durch ihre leeren Zweige sieht
der Himmel, den du hast;
sei Erde jetzt und Abendlied
und Land, darauf er passt.
Demütig sei jetzt wie ein Ding,
zu Wirklichkeit gereift, -
dass Der, von dem die Kunde ging,
dich fühlt, wenn er dich greift.

Mauro Benini, "Judas Holding a Rope and a Sack of Gold"

Whoever is poor at summer's end – as barberries now ripen into red and aged asters breathe weakly in their patch – will ever wait, having lost himself. He knows his wealth of visions, waiting for night's begin to rise up in his darkness, will pass by like an old man for eyes that now cannot close. His days are gone, no more than lies are left to him; to him, even you, God, are like a stone that daily drags him to the deep.	Jetzt reifen schon die roten Berberitzen, alternde Astern atmen schwach im Beet. Wer jetzt nicht reich ist, da der Sommer geht, wird immer warten und sich nie besitzen. Wer jetzt nicht seine Augen schliessen kann, gewiss, dass eine Fülle von Gesichten in ihm nur wartet, bis die Nacht begann, um sich in seinem Dunkel aufzurichten: – der ist vergangen wie ein alter Mann. Dem kommt nichts mehr, dem stösst kein Tag mehr zu, und alles lügt ihn an, was ihm geschieht; auch du, mein Gott. Und wie ein Stein bist du, welcher ihn täglich in die Tiefe zieht.

Heinrich Vogeler, "Women in Mourning"

The kings of the world are old
and will have no heirs.
Their sons die as youths
and their pale daughters
are bequeathed crowns
of sick violence.
Broken small for coin,
the mob – today's world ruler –
turns the gold into machines
that serve their will grudgingly,
and deny them good fortune.
The ore yearns for home,
to leave the coins and wheels,
that teach it nothing of life –
escape the factories and coffers
and return to the veins
of the beckoning mountains,
to be sheltered within.

Die Könige der Welt sind alt
und werden keine Erben haben.
Die Söhne sterben schon als Knaben,
und ihre bleichen Töchter gaben
die kranken Kronen der Gewalt.
Der Pöbel bricht sie klein zu Geld,
der zeitgemässe Herr der Welt
dehnt sie im Feuer zu Maschinen,
die seinem Wollen grollend dienen;
aber das Glück ist nicht mit ihnen.
Das Erz hat Heimweh. Und verlassen
will es die Münzen und die Räder,
die es ein kleines Leben lehren.
Und aus Fabriken und aus Kassen
wird es zurück in das Geäder
der aufgetanen Berge kehren,
die sich verschliessen hinter ihm.

Théo van Rysselberghe, "Big Clouds"

You are the future, great dawn, cock's crow after time's long night, dew on the plains of eternity, morning Matins and the Maid, the mother, the stranger and death. You are the ever-changing form, that emerges always alone from fate, who stays unhailed and unlamented, and unexplored as a forest wild. You are the thing's deeper essence, holding silent the last word of its being, always reflecting one against the other – the ship as the coast and the land as the ship.	Du bist die Zukunft, grosses Morgenrot über den Ebenen der Ewigkeit. Du bist der Hahnschrei nach der Nacht der Zeit, der Tau, die Morgenmette und die Maid, der fremde Mann, die Mutter und der Tod. Du bist die sich verwandelnde Gestalt, Die immer einsam aus dem Schicksal ragt, die unbejubelt bleibt und unbeklagt und unbeschrieben wie ein wilder Wald. Du bist der Dinge tiefer Inbegriff, der seines Wesens letztes Wort verschweigt und sich den andern immer anders zeigt: dem Schiff als Küste und dem Land als Schiff.

"And however much reason I may have to force myself to my writing desk, yet again and again I relent, if the morning suddenly calls me somewhere outside in a way that makes me feel there must be another morning somewhere, a much bigger morning, a morning of seagulls and island birds, a morning of slopes and inaccessible flowers, that same eternal morning that has not yet had to reckon with human beings, who would blink at it noncommittally, distrustfully, and critically in their before-breakfast humour. And one need only walk for half an hour, with those quick, light, early-morning steps that can take one so unimaginably far, to find it truly around one: the sea-morning that is certain everything in it is with it and that nothing opposes it; that in its dawning, its own gesture repeats itself thousands and thousands of times, till it slows down in the small flowers and sums itself up, as it were."

- Letter from RMR to Clara Rilke, 25 February 1907[107]

Paul Cézanne, "Sous-Bois"

I feel this great wonder: *in the world, all life is lived;* and yet everyone is struggling, as if trapped in a prison that hates and holds them. Who lives life then? Is it the thing waiting in the night, like a melody poised on harpstrings? Is it the wind, blown in from the sea – the branches gesturing one to the other? Is it the flowers' scents – the long, aging avenues interwoven? Is it the animals – their fleeting heat – or the birds rising, alien to the earth? Who lives it then? Do you, God – do you live this life?	Und doch, obwohl ein jeder von sich strebt wie aus dem Kerker, der ihn hasst und hält, – es ist ein grosses Wunder in der Welt: ich fühle: alles Leben wird gelebt. Wer lebt es denn? Sind das die Dinge, die wie eine ungespielte Melodie im Abend wie in einer Harfe stehn? Sind das die Winde, die von Wassern wehn, sind das die Zweige, die sich Zeichen geben, sind das die Blumen, die Düfte weben, sind das die langen alternden Alleen? Sind das die warmen Tiere, welche gehn, sind das die Vögel, die sich fremd erheben? Wer lebt es denn? Lebst du es, Gott, – das Leben?

"...Whereupon I remarked that it seemed to me a felicitous sign of progress that the times of the year no longer stand behind us as joyous and mournful backdrops that alternate with indifferent regularity. That we perceive sad Spring seasons and blessed Autumn days full of abundance and joy, that Summer days can be heavy, desolate and unending, and that Winter can touch our feelings like the ring of a triangle, like silver on damask, like roses against a young girl's neck...This is what enables us to live more peacefully and in a deeper understanding with nature, that is, intuitively and without thought. If behind our sorrow a shimmering springtime flickers and moves about in high clouds, then our sadness will be more poignant, and our purple feeling great as it forms wreaths from fallen leaves and uses up all the hues of October, made senseless in their passing."

- Rainer Maria Rilke, The Worpswede Diary, 27 September 1900[108]

Gustav Vigeland, "Gate of Youth"

Gustav Vigeland, "Gate of Youth" and "Column of Life"

You are the heir. Sons are the heirs, for fathers die. Sons stand and blossom. You are the heir.	Du bist der Erbe. Söhne sind die Erben, denn Väter sterben. Söhne stehn und blühn. Du bist der Erbe.

Gustav Vigeland, "Mother and Child"

"One lives so poorly because one always comes into the present unready, impotent and distracted by everything. I can think back on no time in my life without such reproaches and even greater ones. Only during the ten days after Ruth's birth, I think, did I live without deficit; finding reality as indescribable, even in the smallest thing, as it probably always is."

- Letter from RMR to Clara Rilke, 13 September 1907[109]

Vincent van Gogh, "Landscape at St. Remy"

All who seek you, try you and those who find you, bind you, in image and gesture. I would rather know you as the earth knows you; your kingdom growing as I mature. Please engage in no vanity to prove who you are. Time, I know, is different for you. And no prized miracle – instead, give me your righteous laws; more certain are they through the generations.	Alle, welche dich suchen, versuchen dich. Und die, so dich finden, binden dich an Bild und Gebärde. Ich aber will dich begreifen wie dich die Erde begreift; mit meinem Reifen reift dein Reich. Ich will von dir keine Eitelkeit, die dich beweist. Ich weiss, dass die Zeit anders heisst als du. Tu mir kein Wunder zulieb. Gib deinen Gesetzen recht, die von Geschlecht zu Geschlecht sichtbarer sind.

"The sky was a soft gray, with a few bright rips and tears that allowed sunlight through to touch the land on all sides, far and wide. The distances were like biblical scenes with their mountains, groves of trees, and waterways…Of ordinary contour, not any particular locale, simply: the earth. The earth over which the peoples have been scattered like dust in a storm. The earth which is too vast for man in his wanderings, the earth which reaches to the skies and on the other side of the oceans past days and nights begins and grows again, this strange biblical earth, the earth which God still holds in his hands and whose beginning and end thus cannot be seen. The heath stood there black and lusterless, the grass trembling, soft as Japanese silk, metallic red was the mowed buckwheat field, the plowed land dark and heavy."

- Rainer Maria Rilke, The Worpswede Diary, 1 October 1900[110]

Emil Orlik, "Bohemian Village"

In this village stands a last house, solitary as if the world's last house. A street, not deterred by the village, extends slowly out into the night. The small village is just a passage between two worlds – the sensible and the fearful – a path of houses instead of a bridge. And those that leave the village, travel the long pilgrim's road and many, perhaps, die along the way.	In diesem Dorfe steht das letzte Haus so einsam wie das letzte Haus der Welt. Die Strasse, die das kleine Dorf nicht hält, geht langsam weiter in die Nacht hinaus. Das kleine Dorf ist nur ein Übergang zwischen zwei Weiten, ahnungsvoll und bang, ein Weg an Häusern hin statt eines Stegs. Und die das Dorf verlassen, wandern lang, und viele sterben vielleicht unterwegs.

"Already the carriage ride through the glazed hard Autumn afternoon and the primitive countryside was so beautiful. I drove alone from the train and back to the train. And that was Bohemia as I knew it, hills rolling like light music and suddenly level again behind apple trees, flat without much horizon and divided by fields and rows of trees, like a folk song from refrain to refrain…"

- Letter from RMR to Clara Rilke, 4 November 1907[111]

Ernst Barlach, "Desert Preacher"

O God, if only I were many pilgrims –
forming a long train moving towards you –
I could become an even bigger part of you
and walk your garden of living paths.
If I only go as I am, alone –
will they notice me then –
see me as I go to you – be moved,
and turn eagerly back to you?

But they would only laugh,
as if there were no line of pilgrims.
So I am happy to go as I am –
unseen by those that scoff.

Du Gott, ich möchte viele Pilger sein,
um so, ein langer Zug, zu dir zu gehn,
und um ein grosses Stück von dir zu sein:
du Garten mit den lebenden Alleen.
Wenn ich so gehe, wie ich bin, allein, –
wer merkt es denn? Wer sieht mich zu dir gehn?
Wen reisst es hin? Wen regt es auf, und wen
bekehrt es dir?

   Als wäre nichts geschehn,
– lachen sie weiter. Und da bin ich froh,
dass ich so gehe wie ich bin; denn so
kann keiner von den Lachenden mich sehn.

Honoré-Victorin Daumier, "Fugitives" or "Emigrants"

As when one dies
and the body is carried out,
the houses know no peace –
so one hears the secret call,
puts on the collar
and travels to a foreign land;
taking the pilgrim's staff,
he seeks the way, knowing
he will find you there.

The ways will never be clear
of those that seek you like the rose
that blooms once every thousand years.
So they finally reach you,
tired and almost nameless in the dark.

But when I saw them on the plains,
so great was the train of their passage,
that since then, I believe that their cloaks
stirred up the wind as they moved
and stilled it as they encamped.

Es wird nicht Ruhe in den Häusern, sei's,
dass einer stirbt und sie ihn weitertragen,
sei es, dass wer auf heimliches Geheiss
den Pilgerstock nimmt und den Pilgerkragen,
um in der Fremde nach dem Weg zu fragen,
auf welchem er dich warten weiss.

Die Strassen werden derer niemals leer,
die zu dir wollen wie zu jener Rose,
die alle tausend Jahre einmal blüht.
Viel dunkles Volk und beinah Namenlose,
und wenn sie dich erreichen, sind sie müd.

Aber ich habe ihren Zug gesehn;
und glaube seither, dass die Winde wehn
aus ihren Mänteln, welche sich bewegen,
und stille sind wenn sie sich niederlegen –:
so gross war in den Ebenen ihr Gehn.

Gustav Vigeland, "Old Man" and the "Tower of Life"

God, you also will be great.
Greater than anyone living can imagine.
More aged than an old man,
you remain still unfamiliar and unique.

Like a fragrance from a nearby garden,
one will sense you – *love you* –
with trepidation and tenderness,
just as a sick man clings
to his favorite things.

There will be no prayers
that the people chant together –
you are not found in assembly.
Those who rejoice and delight in you
will be like the last man on earth,
cast out, but not alone,
misspent, but not lost,
tear-stained, but laughing,
house-small, but mighty as a kingdom.

Auch du wirst gross sein. Grösser noch, als einer,
der jetzt schon leben muss, dich sagen kann.
Viel ungewöhnlicher und ungemeiner
und noch viel älter als ein alter Mann.

Man wird dich fühlen: dass ein Duften ginge
aus eines Gartens naher Gegenwart;
und wie ein Kranker seine liebsten Dinge
wird man dich lieben ahnungsvoll und zart.

Es wird kein Beten geben, das die Leute
zusammenschart. Du bist nicht im Verein;
und wer dich fühlte und sich an dir freute,
wird wie der Einzige auf Erden sein:
Ein Ausgestossener und ein Vereinter,
gesammelt und vergeudet doch zugleich;
ein Lächelnder und doch ein Halbverweinter,
klein wie ein Haus und mächtig wie ein Reich.

"First one has to find God somewhere, experience Him as so infinitely, so vastly, so enormously present; that whatever one feels toward Him – be it fear, be it astonishment, be it breathlessness, be it finally love – it really hardly matters. But religion – a coercion to God – there is no place for that if one has started with the discovery of God; there is then no stopping any more, no matter at whatever point one may have begun." –Letter from RMR to Ilse Blumenthal-Weiss, 18 December 1921[112]

Otto Modersohn, "On the Bank of the Moor"

By day, like hearsay,
you flow in whispers among the many;
after the sounding of the hour,
you are the silence, slowly growing.

The more the day inclines to night
with ever weaker gestures,
the more you are with us, my God.
Your kingdom rises above us
like smoke from all the rooftops.

Bei Tag bist du das Hörensagen,
das flüsternd um die vielen fliesst;
die Stille nach dem Stundenschlagen,
welche sich langsam wieder schliesst.

Je mehr der Tag mit immer schwächern
Gebärden sich nach Abend neigt,
je mehr bist du, mein Gott. Es steigt
dein Reich wie Rauch aus allen Dächern.

Auguste Rodin, "The Cry"

I pray again, Illustrious One – Let my words, born deep within me, resound in power and reach you through the wind. Enemies divided me up; I am scattered in pieces. O God, I was drowned in their laughter and they drank me down. I reassembled myself in courtyards from refuse and old glass; half-dumb, I stammered my prayer to you, raised my half-hands to you in wordless supplication, pleading for lost eyes, with which to see you, eternal symmetry. I was like a burnt-down house, sometimes refuge for murderers before they resumed their ravenous, punishing hunts through the land; I was like a city by the sea, assaulted by plague, that like a heavy corpse, pulled on the children's hands. I was as much a stranger to myself as anyone; of him, I knew only of the pain he caused my young mother, her heart constricted, pressed painfully upon me, in her womb.	Ich bete wieder, du Erlauchter, du hörst mich wieder durch den Wind, weil meine Tiefen nie gebrauchter rauschender Worte mächtig sind. Ich war zerstreut; an Widersacher in Stücken war verteilt mein Ich. O Gott, mich lachten alle Lacher und alle Trinker tranken mich. In Höfen hab ich mich gesammelt aus Abfall und aus altem Glas, mit halbem Mund dich angestammelt, dich, Ewiger aus Ebenmass. Wie hob ich meine halben Hände zu dir in namenlosem Flehn, dass ich die Augen wiederfände, mit denen ich dich angesehn. Ich war ein Haus nach einem Brand, darin nur Mörder manchmal schlafen, eh ihre hungerigen Strafen sie weiterjagen in das Land; ich war wie eine Stadt am Meer, wenn eine Seuche sie bedrängte, die sich wie eine Leiche schwer den Kindern an die Hände hängte. Ich war mir fremd wie irgendwer, und wusste nur von ihm, dass er einst meine junge Mutter kränkte, als sie mich trug, und dass ihr Herz, das eingeengte, sehr schmerzhaft an mein Keimen schlug. (continued on next page)

Constantin Emile Meunier, "La Glebe (The Earth)"

Now I am whole again, built up from all the pieces of my shame, but longing for an understanding - a singular tie between us, a bond that grasps me - as if I were *a thing* - with the great hands of your heart: (O would that they reached me) I number myself, my God, and you, you have the right to spend me.	Jetzt bin ich wieder aufgebaut aus allen Stücken meiner Schande, und sehne mich nach einem Bande, nach einem einigen Verstande, der mich wie ein Ding überschaut, – nach deines Herzens grossen Händen – (o kämen sie doch auf mich zu) ich zähle mich, mein Gott, und du, du hast das Recht, mich zu verschwenden.

"Ah, we measure the years and cut off here and there and stop and begin and pause between the two. But how very much of one piece is everything we encounter, how related one thing is to the next, how it gives birth to itself and grows up and is schooled in its own nature, and all we have to do essentially is to *be there*, but unpretentiously, urgently, the way the earth simply is, acquiescent in the seasons, light and dark and suspended in space, not asking to rest upon anything other than the web of influences and powers in which the stars themselves feel secure."

- Letter from RMR to Clara Rilke, 19 October 1907[113]

Hieronymus Bosch,
"Death and the Miser"

Do not be troubled, God.
They say *mine* for all things,
that are unresisting.
They are like the wind
that blows across the branches
and says: *my* tree

They hardly notice
how everything glows
that you grasp
and that they could not touch
the hem of your cloak
without burning.

They say *mine,* just as one
might freely claim a prince as friend
when talking to a farmer,
if the prince is great – and far away.
They say *mine* of their strange walls
and have no clue of their home's real master.
They say *mine* to name each possession,
as a charlatan might say that
the sun and lightning were his to command;
but each thing closes at their approach.
So they say: my life, my wife,
my dog, my child and yet truly know,
that it all – life, wife, dog and child
are images apart from them
that they can only blindly nudge
with outstretched hands.
Admittedly, this certainty
may be only with those few
who greatly yearn to see.
For the others have no ears
to hear that they wander,
poor and bereft of things,
that they can no more *possess* a wife
than they could the flowers;
an alienated life is theirs,
spurned by their possessions.

Du musst nicht bangen, Gott. Sie sagen: mein
zu allen Dingen, die geduldig sind.
Sie sind wie Wind, der an die Zweige streift
und sagt: mein Baum.

Sie merken kaum,
wie alles glüht, was ihre Hand ergreift, –
so dass sie's auch an seinem letzten Saum
nicht halten könnten, ohne zu verbrennen.

Sie sagen mein, wie manchmal einer gern
den Fürsten Freund nennt im Gespräch mit Bauern,
wenn dieser Fürst sehr gross ist und – sehr fern.
Sie sagen mein von ihren fremden Mauern
und kennen gar nicht ihres Hauses Herrn.
Sie sagen mein und nennen das Besitz,
wenn jedes Ding sich schliesst, dem sie sich nahn,
so wie ein abgeschmackter Scharlatan
vielleicht die Sonne sein nennt und den Blitz.
So sagen sie: mein Leben, meine Frau,
mein Hund, mein Kind, und wissen doch genau,
dass alles: Leben, Frau und Hund und Kind
fremde Gebilde sind, daran sie blind
mit ihren ausgestreckten Händen stossen.
Gewissheit freilich ist das nur den Grossen,
die sich nach Augen sehnen. Denn die Andern
wollen's nicht hören, dass ihr armes Wandern
mit keinem Dinge rings zusammenhängt,
dass sie, von ihrer Habe fortgedrängt,
nicht anerkannt von ihrem Eigentume,
das Weib so wenig haben wie die Blume,
die eines fremden Lebens ist für alle.

(continued on next page)

Hieronymus Bosch, "The Conjurer"

Do not fall out of balance, God.
Even he who loves you –
who knows your countenance
in the dark, wavering
like a light in your breath –
cannot possess you.
And if in the night
one captures you in his prayer:
 	
    You are the guest,
    who goes far away again.
 	
Who can hold you, God?
For you are yours alone,
possessed by no hand,
just as a maturing wine
becomes ever sweeter
as it possesses itself.
	Falle nicht, Gott, aus deinem Gleichgewicht.
	Auch der dich liebt und der dein Angesicht
	erkennt im Dunkel, wenn er wie ein Licht
	in deinem Atem schwankt, – besitzt dich nicht.
	Und wenn dich einer in der Nacht erfasst,
	so dass du kommen musst in sein Gebet:
	
	    Du bist der Gast,
	    der wieder weitergeht.
	
	Wer kann dich halten, Gott? Denn du bist dein,
	von keines Eigentümers Hand gestört,
	so wie der noch nicht ausgereifte Wein,
	der immer süsser wird, sich selbst gehört.

"One must never despair over having lost something – a person, a joy or a happiness; everything comes back again more wonderful. What must fall away, falls away; what belongs to us stays with us, for everything proceeds according to laws that are greater than our understanding and with which we are only seemingly at odds. One must live in oneself and think of the entirety of life, of all its millions of possibilities, distances, and futures, in the face of which nothing is past and lost."

- Letter from RMR to Friedrich Westhoff, 29 April 1904[114]

"…here and there are painters searching for motifs, painters who break five small stones out of the great mosaic in order to combine them into some harmony. And perhaps it is not only painters who are like that…perhaps people in general do that as well –: have they not built their lives out of little motifs, are not their joys and their travails, their professions and wealth merely motifs?...a true life is like the real world. And lies there like a pasture in the evening, gifting warm breath and scent and the absence of people…"

- Letter from RMR to Clara Rilke, 29 July 1904[115]

Auguste Rodin, "Prodigal Son" or "Prayer"

In deepest night, I dig for you, you treasure. For all known excess of wealth is as poverty and a paltry substitute for your inchoate beauty. But the way to you is terribly far and dissipated by the winds of time, having been too long neglected. O, you are alone. You are loneliness itself, you heart that travels to valleys remote. I raise my hands into the wind, open and bloody with digging, my fingers outstretched like branches to pluck the pieces of you from the air; as if you had been shattered by an impatient gesture – had fallen from distant stars back to our world, atomized and soft as a Spring rain.	In tiefen Nächten grab ich dich, du Schatz. Denn alle Überflüsse, die ich sah, sind Armut und armseliger Ersatz für deine Schönheit, die noch nie geschah. Aber der Weg zu dir ist furchtbar weit und, weil ihn lange keiner ging, verweht. O du bist einsam. Du bist Einsamkeit, du Herz, das zu entfernten Talen geht. Und meine Hände, welche blutig sind vom Graben, heb ich offen in den Wind, so dass sie sich verzweigen wie ein Baum. Ich sauge dich mit ihnen aus dem Raum, als hättest du dich einmal dort zerschellt in einer ungeduldigen Gebärde, und fielest jetzt, eine zerstäubte Welt, aus fernen Sternen wieder auf die Erde sanft wie ein Frühlingsregen fällt.

"Such is the slender youth kneeling with arms flung up and backward in a gesture of unlimited invocation. Rodin called this figure, *The Prodigal Son*, but – who knows from where – it assumes the name of *Prayer*. And it soon outgrows that name as well. This is not a son kneeling before his father. This posture makes a God necessary, and in this kneeling figure are present all who need Him. This marble harkens to all distances; it is alone in the world." – Rainer Maria Rilke, Monograph on Auguste Rodin[116]

Käthe Kollwitz, "In God's Hands"

Blind me - I see you still, hear you, even though made deaf. Take away my feet and mouth, and yet I run to give my oath to you. Break off my arms – I yet reach for you, my heart holding you like a hand - even if you stop my heart, my brain would beat instead, and if then you set my brain ablaze, I would serve you with my blood.	Lösch mir die Augen aus: ich kann dich sehn, wirf mir die Ohren zu: ich kann dich hören, und ohne Füsse kann ich zu dir gehn, und ohne Mund noch kann ich dich beschwören. Brich mir die Arme ab, ich fasse dich mit meinem Herzen wie mit einer Hand, halt mir das Herz zu, und mein Hirn wird schlagen, und wirfst du in mein Hirn den Brand, so werd ich dich auf meinem Blute tragen.

Auguste Rodin, "La Douleur (de la Porte)"

And my soul is like a woman before you,
with a bond like Ruth's to Naomi.
By day, as a faithful servant,
she bundles up your sheaves.
But in the evening, when all is still
she bathes in the incoming tide
and puts on her best dress;
she comes to you, when all is still around you
she comes and uncovers your feet.
And if you ask her in the middle of night,
she replies with deep simplicity:
I am Ruth, your servant.
Stretch your wings over me.
You are the heir…

And until daylight breaks,
My soul sleeps at your feet,
warmed by your blood,
and is a like a woman before you.
and is like Ruth.

Und meine Seele ist ein Weib vor dir.
Und ist wie der Naëmi Schnur, wie Ruth.
Sie geht bei Tag um deiner Garben Hauf
wie eine Magd, die tiefe Dienste tut.
Aber am Abend steigt sie in die Flut
und badet sich und kleidet sich sehr gut
und kommt zu dir, wenn alles um dich ruht,
und kommt und deckt zu deinen Füssen auf.
Und fragst du sie um Mitternacht, sie sagt
mit tiefer Einfalt: Ich bin Ruth, die Magd.
Spann deine Flügel über deine Magd.
Du bist der Erbe …

Und meine Seele schläft dann, bis es tagt,
bei deinen Füssen, warm von deinem Blut.
Und ist ein Weib vor dir. Und ist wie Ruth.

William Blake, "Job's Tormentors"

"And the LORD said to Satan, 'Have you considered my servant Job, that there is none like him on the earth, a blameless and upright man, who fears God and turns away from evil?'… Then Satan answered the LORD…'But put forth your hand now, and touch all that he has, and he will curse you to your face.'"

– Book of Job 1:8-11

OFFICE OF THE DEAD

VESPERS

(Sunset)

Auguste Rodin, "Large Clenched Hand with Figure"

I am so deep, I see no future – perhaps, like an isolated, hard vein of ore, I move through heavy mountains and can see no end of rock; it all presses in on me and everything near has become stone. I am no master of pain, so this great darkness makes me small; but if you are there; be heavy as well and let your whole hand break through to me and my cry break though to you.	Vielleicht, dass ich durch schwere Berge gehe in harten Adern, wie ein Erz allein; und bin so tief, dass ich kein Ende sehe und keine Ferne: alles wurde Nähe, und alle Nähe wurde Stein. Ich bin ja noch kein Wissender im Wehe, – so macht mich dieses grosse Dunkel klein; bist du es aber: mach dich schwer, brich ein: dass deine ganze Hand an mir geschehe und ich an dir mit meinem ganzen Schrein.

"I reproach all modern religions for only having supplied their followers with consolations and euphemisms for death, instead of arming them with the disposition needed to endure and come to an understanding with death. With it, with its full, unmasked savagery: a cruelty that is so enormous that it is just within it that the circle closes…like the moon, life certainly has a side always turned away from us which is not life's counter-part, but its supplement for completeness, towards full presence, to the really sound and full sphere and globe of existence…Only because we exclude death in a summary contemplation, has it turned more and more into something alien, and as we have held it at a distance, something hostile…Life always says simultaneously Yes and No. Indeed, Death…is the true yea-sayer. It says only: Yes. Before eternity." –Letter from RMR to Countess Margot Sizzo, 6 January 1923.[117]

Käthe Kollwitz, "Welcoming Death"

O Lord, grant each their own unique death – a death growing, in meaning and need, out of all in life that that they loved.	O Herr, gib jedem seinen eignen Tod, das Sterben, das aus jenem Leben geht, darin er Liebe hatte, Sinn und Not.

"I created a new form of caress: to place a rose softly on a closed eye, until its coolness barely can be felt any longer and only the gentleness of its petal still rests on the lid, like sleep before sunrise."

- Rainer Maria Rilke, The Worpswede Diary, 27 September 1900[118]

"…oceans, parks, forests and forest meadows: my longing for these is sometimes indescribable. Now, that Winter already threatens here. These foggy mornings and evenings already have begun, where the sun is merely the place where the sun was earlier, and where in the yards all the summer flowers, the dahlias, the big gladiolas and long rows of geraniums all cry out the contradiction of their red into the mist. This makes me sad. It brings up dreary memories, one doesn't know why; as if the music of the city's Summer were ending in dissonance, in a revolt of all its notes; perhaps just because one already once before has interpreted and taken all this deep into oneself and bound it to oneself, without ever actually doing it."

- Letter from RMR to Clara Rilke, 13 September 1907[119]

Epitaph written by Rainer Maria Rilke for his tombstone, 1926[120]:

"ROSE, OH REINER WIDERSPRUCH,
                                      LUST,
NIEMANDES SCHLAF ZU SEIN
                        UNTER SOVIEL
LIDERN."

"Rose, oh pure contradiction, desire,
no one's sleep to be, under so many lids."

Arnold Böcklin, "Isle of the Dead"

"...by regarding God and Death as not having presence in Life (as being otherworldly, coming later, existing elsewhere, different), one has hastened the shrinking of the cycle of the here and now even more; this so-called progress became the happening of a self-impressed world which had forgotten that, already from the start, it was surpassed by Death and by God, no matter how hard it tried... Nature does not accept this somehow successful displacement of ours - when a tree begins to bud, Death blossoms within it as much as Life. The fallow field is full of Death, having cast off its rich expression of Life, and the animals walk patiently from one to the other. All around us, Death is still at home, and from within the cracks of things it observes us, and a rusty nail, somewhere protruding from a board, does nothing but rejoice over it day and night."

- Letter from RMR to Lotte Hepner, 8 November 1915[121]

The great death is in each us –
all revolves around this fruit
and we are just its rind and leaf.

For its sake, girls blossom
like trees from lutes
and boys mature into men;
women are confidantes
to those who grow,
for worries that otherwise
one could not bear.
For its sake –
for each who paints and builds –
there was a world around this fruit;
turning to it, freezing and thawing,
they look – and the watched stays
as if eternal, even though long past.
All the warmth of the heart
and the white glow of the mind
have filled it throughout –:
and your angels,
descending like a flock of birds,
made all the fruits green.

Denn wir sind nur die Schale und das Blatt.
Der grosse Tod, den jeder in sich hat,
das ist die Frucht, um die sich alles dreht.

Um ihretwillen heben Mädchen an
und kommen wie ein Baum aus einer Laute,
und Knaben sehnen sich um sie zum Mann;
und Frauen sind den Wachsenden Vertraute
für Ängste, die sonst niemand nehmen kann.
Um ihretwillen bleibt das Angeschaute
wie Ewiges, auch wenn es lang verrann, –
und jeder, welcher bildete und baute,
ward Welt um diese Frucht, und fror und taute
und windete ihr zu und schien sie an.
In sie ist eingegangen alle Wärme,
der Herzen und der Hirne weisses Glühn –:
Doch deine Engel ziehn wie Vogelschwärme,
und sie erfanden alle Früchte grün.

Ernst Barlach, "Death in Life"

The big cities are not true - with the things that are willing, they deceive the day and night, animals and the child; their noises and even their silences are lies. None of that which is truly real, which widely moves around you, expectant one, can be found in them. In their alleys, the rush of your blowing wind - it passes also over flowerbeds and avenues - is turned this way and that – irritated, agitated and confused.	Die grossen Städte sind nicht wahr; sie täuschen den Tag, die Nacht, die Tiere und das Kind; ihr Schweigen lügt, sie lügen mit Geräuschen und mit den Dingen, welche willig sind. Nichts von dem weiten wirklichen Geschehen, das sich um dich, du Werdender, bewegt, geschieht in ihnen. Deiner Winde Wehen fällt in die Gassen, die es anders drehen, ihr Rauschen wird im Hin- und Wiedergehen verwirrt, gereizt und aufgeregt. Sie kommen auch zu Beeten und Alleen –:

"… Paris was an experience for me not unlike that of the military school; for just as then a great anxious astonishment gripped me, so now I was gripped by fright at everything that in some unspeakable confusion is called life…the carriages drove straight at me, full of disdain, as if driving over a bad place in which stale water has collected. And often before going to sleep I read the thirtieth chapter of the Book of Job, and it was all true for me, word for word.

…And once late in Autumn a little old woman stood beside me one evening in the light of a store window. She stood very still, and I thought that like me she was occupied looking at the goods displayed in the window, and so I hardly paid any attention to her. Finally, though, I began to feel uneasy in her presence; and, I don't know why, I suddenly looked down at her oddly folded, worn hands. Very, very slowly an old, long, thin pencil emerged from those hands; it grew and grew and took a very long time before it became totally visible, visible in all of its wretchedness. I can't say exactly what it was that made this scene so appalling, but it seemed to me as if a whole destiny were being played out before me, a long fate, a catastrophe that was building up fearfully to the moment when the pencil would cease to grow and, trembling ever so slightly, fall from the loneliness of those empty hands. I understood finally that I was supposed to buy it."

- Letter from RMR to Lou Andreas-Salomé, 18 July 1903[122]

MATINS
(Midnight)

Ernst Barlach, "Russian Beggar Woman"

They are not poor. They are just the not-rich, possessing no will and no world; marked with the sign of ultimate fear, over all disfigured and leafless. All of the cities' dust clings to them and the filth cleaves to them. They are shunned like discarded potsherds, like skeletons on pox-infested beds, and discarded like a calendar for a past year – and yet, if the earth were in need, it would array the poor like a necklace ringed with roses and wear them as a talisman. For the poor, more pure than unflawed stone, wish for nothing and need only *one thing* – like a new-born animal, eyes yet to open and full of simplicity and unending Yours – allow them to be as poor as they really are. For poverty is a great splendor from within…	Sie sind es nicht. Sie sind nur die Nicht-Reichen, die ohne Willen sind und ohne Welt; gezeichnet mit der letzten Ängste Zeichen und überall entblättert und entstellt. Zu ihnen drängt sich aller Staub der Städte, und aller Unrat hängt sich an sie an. Sie sind verrufen wie ein Blatternbette, wie Scherben fortgeworfen, wie Skelette, wie ein Kalender, dessen Jahr verrann, – und doch: wenn deine Erde Nöte hätte: sie reihte sie an eine Rosenkette und trüge sie wie einen Talisman. Denn sie sind reiner als die reinen Steine und wie das blinde Tier, das erst beginnt, und voller Einfalt und unendlich deine und wollen nichts und brauchen nur das eine: so arm sein dürfen, wie sie wirklich sind. Denn Armut ist ein grosser Glanz aus Innen …

"And he lifted up his eyes on his disciples, and said:
'Blessed are you poor, for yours is the kingdom of God.
Blessed are you that hunger now, for you shall be satisfied.
Blessed are you that weep now, for you shall laugh.'"

- Luke 6:20-21

Ernst Barlach, "The Blind Beggar"

You who know, and whose knowledge is born from poverty and a surfeit of poverty: make it so, that the poor are no longer thrown down and stepped on in frustration. While others are rootless, the poor stand like a display of melissa, firm in their roots, their leaves jagged and tender, giving off a lemon scent.	Du, der du weisst, und dessen weites Wissen aus Armut ist und Armutsüberfluss: Mach, dass die Armen nichtmehr fortgeschmissen und eingetreten werden in Verdruss. Die andern Menschen sind wie ausgerissen; sie aber stehn wie eine Blumenart aus Wurzeln auf und duften wie Melissen und ihre Blätter sind gezackt und zart.

Ernst Barlach, "Woman in the Wind"

Consider them and see what they resemble: they move as if stirred by the wind and rest like something one holds. In their eyes is a meadow at dusk, striped with the darkening lines of day, on which a sudden summer rain falls.	Betrachte sie und sieh, was ihnen gliche: sie rühren sich wie in den Wind gestellt und ruhen aus wie etwas, was man hält. In ihren Augen ist das feierliche Verdunkeltwerden lichter Wiesenstriche, auf die ein rascher Sommerregen fällt.

"After the bustle of the city to see these high waiting woods again! How refined this stand of trees is, this calm. Bewildered by the agitated gestures of human beings, one comes to feel that there are only two related and great movements. The beating of wings of a bird high above and the swaying of the treetops. These two gestures are meant to teach your soul how to move."

- Rainer Maria Rilke, The Schmargendorf Diary, 7 April 1900[123]

Emil Orlik, "Woman Gathering Wood in the Forest"

They are so quiet; almost like things. And if you invite them in, they are like returning friends, leaving humbly, then lost and darkening like a unused tool. They are like imposed guardians of treasure – a boat carried up from the depths, then spread out and opened as one would ready a linen for bleaching – a treasure they protect, but never see themselves.	Sie sind so still; fast gleichen sie den Dingen. Und wenn man sich sie in die Stube lädt, sind sie wie Freunde, die sich wiederbringen, und gehn verloren unter dem Geringen und dunkeln wie ein ruhiges Gerät. Sie sind wie Wächter bei verhängten Schätzen, die sie bewahren, aber selbst nicht sahn, – getragen von den Tiefen wie ein Kahn, und wie das Leinen auf den Bleicheplätzen so ausgebreitet und so aufgetan.

Ernst Barlach, "The Abandoned Ones"

And see how their feet are alive;
like the tracks of animals,
interlaced hundredfold
on each path; full of memories
of stone and snow and of the
gentle, freshly cooled meadows,
over which they went.

They take part in that great suffering,
from which men fell to their lesser sorrows;
they embrace their fates
like fingers plucking strings –
the balm of grass and cutting edge of stone –
walking across the meadows in your eyes.

Und sieh, wie ihrer Füsse Leben geht:
wie das der Tiere, hundertfach verschlungen
mit jedem Wege; voll Erinnerungen
an Stein und Schnee und an die leichten, jungen
gekühlten Wiesen, über die es weht.

Sie haben Leid von jenem grossen Leide,
aus dem der Mensch zu kleinem Kummer fiel;
des Grases Balsam und der Steine Schneide
ist ihnen Schicksal, – und sie lieben beide
und gehen wie auf deiner Augen Weide
und so wie Hände gehn im Saitenspiel.

Käthe Kollwitz, "Praying Woman"

And their hands are like a woman's, / warm to the touch and quietly trusting, / as fitted for a kind of motherhood / as a drinking vessel is shaped to the hand, / as serene as birds building their nests.	Und ihre Hände sind wie die von Frauen, / und irgendeiner Mutterschaft gemäss; / so heiter wie die Vögel wenn sie bauen, – / im Fassen warm und ruhig im Vertrauen, / und anzufühlen wie ein Trinkgefäss.

Auguste Rodin, "Head of a Girl"

Their mouth is like the mouth of a bust, that never uttered sound, breathed or kissed; and yet is wisely formed, arched as if it knew it all, received from a past life and yet is just a likeness – stone, a thing…	Ihr Mund ist wie der Mund an einer Büste, der nie erklang und atmete und küsste und doch aus einem Leben das verging, das alles, weise eingeformt, empfing, und sich nun wölbt, als ob er alles wüsste – und doch nur Gleichnis ist und Stein und Ding…

Dreamer Sculpture, Chartres Cathedral, Chartres, France

"In the first year of Belshaz'zar king of Babylon, Daniel had a dream and visions of his head as he lay in his bed. Then he wrote down the dream and told the sum of the matter. Daniel said, 'I saw in my vision by night, and behold, the four winds of heaven were stirring up the great sea. And four great beasts came up out of the sea, different from one another…

As I looked, thrones were placed
and one that was ancient of days took his seat;
his clothing was white as snow,
and the hair of his head like pure wool;
his throne was fiery flames,
its wheels were burning fire.
A stream of fire issued
and came forth from before him;
a thousand thousands served him,
and ten thousand times ten thousand stood before him;
the court sat in judgment,
and the books were opened.'"

Daniel 7: 1-10

And their voice arrives from the distance, but sets off before sunrise, for weeks it roamed the great forests and having seen the sea, from the sea it spoke to Daniel in his dream.	Und ihre Stimme kommt von ferneher und ist vor Sonnenaufgang aufgebrochen und war in grossen Wäldern, geht seit Wochen und hat im Schlaf mit Daniel gesprochen und hat das Meer gesehn, und sagt vom Meer.

Ernst Barlach, "Sleeping Peasant Couple"

And when they sleep, at midnight
and at dawn, scattered, like bread
apportioned widely during a famine,
they are as a rain in the fallen darkness,
returning to all the fertility of youth,
which had been silently lent.
There remains then no scar
on their body, no name embedded,
like the seed of that seed
from which you will come in eternity.

Und wenn sie schlafen, sind sie wie an alles
zurückgegeben was sie leise leiht,
und weit verteilt wie Brot in Hungersnöten
an Mitternächte und an Morgenröten,
und sind wie Regen voll des Niederfalles
in eines Dunkels junge Fruchtbarkeit.
Dann bleibt nicht eine Narbe ihres Namens
auf ihrem Leib zurück, der keimbereit
sich bettet wie der Samen jenes Samens,
aus dem du stammen wirst von Ewigkeit.

Auguste Rodin, "The Age of Bronze"

And see: their body is like a bridgroom's, so passionate and wonderful, a handsome object so full of life, even at rest, it flows like a brook. Women's frailties and worries are gathered up in his slender frame; yet he is strong in his manhood- a dragon, asleep in shame's valley, waiting.	Und sieh: ihr Leib ist wie ein Bräutigam und fliesst im Liegen hin gleich einem Bache, und lebt so schön wie eine schöne Sache, so leidenschaftlich und so wundersam. In seiner Schlankheit sammelt sich das Schwache, das Bange, das aus vielen Frauen kam; doch sein Geschlecht ist stark und wie ein Drache und wartet schlafend in dem Tal der Scham.

"Here was a life-sized statue ["The Age of Bronze"] showing life which was not only equally powerful in every part but which was, as it seemed, raised everywhere to the height of the same expression… It was as if this man's power rose from deep within the earth. This was the silhouette of a tree that still has the March storms ahead of it and is anxious because the fruit and fullness of its summer no longer lived within the roots, but already, slowly rising, stands in the trunk around which the great winds will hunt. The figure is important from another point of view. It marks the birth of gesture in Rodin's work. The gesture that grew and gradually developed into such greatness and power, here it flowed forth like a spring, which softly descended upon this body… Reluctantly, it dissolves itself in the raised arms; and those arms are still so heavy that the hand of one is resting again at the top of the head. But sleep has been cast off and power is gathering itself…And in the right foot the first step awaits." – Rainer Maria Rilke, Monograph on Rodin[124]

Ernst Barlach, "Wanderers"

For look: they will live and multiply,
undefeated by time,
flourishing like wild berries
that cover the forest floor
under a carpet of sweetness.

Blessed are those, who are in no way remote
and who, roofless, stand at peace in the rain;
the harvest entire shall be their reward
and their fruit will increase thousand-fold.

They will survive each era and kingdom
whose meaning will be lost to time
and like rested hands, will rise up,
while the hands of all other classes
and peoples will be exhausted.

Denn sieh: sie werden leben und sich mehren
und nicht bezwungen werden von der Zeit
und werden wachsen wie des Waldes Beeren
den Boden bergend unter Süssigkeit.

Denn selig sind, die niemals sich entfernten
und still im Regen standen ohne Dach;
zu ihnen werden kommen alle Ernten,
und ihre Frucht wird voll sein tausendfach.

Sie werden dauern über jedes Ende
und über Reiche, deren Sinn verrinnt,
und werden sich wie ausgeruhte Hände
erheben, wenn die Hände aller Stände
und aller Völker müde sind.

Paul Gauguin, "Christmas Night (The Blessing of the Oxen)"

Only take them back
from the sinful cities,
where all is anger and confusion,
where the tumult of the days
wither them in wounded patience.

Does the earth have no room for them?
For whom does the wind search?
Who drinks the shining of the brook?
In the ponds' deep dream of the shore,
is there no reflection left
for door and threshold?
Like a tree, the poor
need only a small place
where they can have it all.

Nur nimm sie wieder aus der Städte Schuld,
wo ihnen alles Zorn ist und verworren
und wo sie in den Tagen aus Tumult
verdorren mit verwundeter Geduld.

Hat denn für sie die Erde keinen Raum?
Wen sucht der Wind? Wer trinkt des Baches Helle?
Ist in der Teiche tiefem Ufertraum
kein Spiegelbild mehr frei für Tür und Schwelle?
Sie brauchen ja nur eine kleine Stelle,
auf der sie alles haben wie ein Baum.

LAUDS

(Dawn)

Auguste Rodin, "Memorial Relief (Hand of a Child)"

The home of the poor is like an altar-shrine. In it, the eternal is transformed into sustenance, and when evening tolls, like an echo it turns back in a wide circle and enters slowly back into itself. The home of the poor is like an altar-shrine. The home of the poor is like a child's hand. It spurns what adults desire, and like the swaying pan on a suspended scale, it values what is received– a beetle ornamentally pincered, a stone rounded smooth in a creek, sand running through fingers and shells that give sound. The home of the poor is like a child's hand. And the home of the poor is like the earth. Warm as the poverty warmth of a stable; a fragment of a future crystal, it is now light, then dark in its tumbling fall; – and yet the nights are: they are everything, and all of the stars enter through the gates of the night.	Des Armen Haus ist wie ein Altarschrein, drin wandelt sich das Ewige zur Speise, und wenn der Abend kommt, so kehrt es leise zu sich zurück in einem weiten Kreise und geht voll Nachklang langsam in sich ein. Des Armen Haus ist wie ein Altarschrein. Des Armen Haus ist wie des Kindes Hand. Sie nimmt nicht, was Erwachsene verlangen; nur einen Käfer mit verzierten Zangen, den runden Stein, der durch den Bach gegangen, den Sand, der rann, und Muscheln, welche klangen; sie ist wie eine Waage aufgehangen und sagt das allerleiseste Empfangen langschwankend an mit ihrer Schalen Stand. Des Armen Haus ist wie des Kindes Hand. Und wie die Erde ist des Armen Haus: Der Splitter eines künftigen Kristalles, bald licht, bald dunkel in der Flucht des Falles; arm wie die warme Armut eines Stalles, – und doch sind Abende: da ist sie alles, und alle Sterne gehen von ihr aus.

"So it comes to be that most people have no idea how beautiful the world is and how much splendor reveals itself in the smallest things, in some flower, a stone, the bark of a tree, or a birch leaf…the finest thing would be if all people wished always to stay in this relationship like mindful and good children, with simple and pious feelings, and if they would not lose the ability to rejoice as deeply in a birch leaf, in the feather of a peacock or the wing of a hooded crow as in a great mountain range or a resplendent palace. The small is as little small as the large – is large. There is a great and eternal beauty throughout the entire world, and it is distributed equitably over all things great and small; for in the important and essential there is no inequity on the whole earth." –Letter from RMR to Helmuth Westhoff, 12 November 1901[125]

Édouard Vuillard, "Une Gallerie au Gymnase"

The cities only want what they want / and tear up all in their path. / They break up animals like hollow wood / and consume the nations in the flames. / / And their people are slaves to a culture / that deems their snail tracks progress; / falling deeply out of balance and measure, / they plunge ahead, where they used to go slow / - metal and glass loudly screeching - / with the sentiments and glare of whores. / / It is as if they daily ape an illusion, / for they can no longer be themselves; / the power of gold, great as the east wind, / grows at their expense and makes them small, / holds them at bay, until the wine / and all the poisons of animals and humanity / tempt them into idle pursuits.	Die Städte aber wollen nur das Ihre / und reissen alles mit in ihren Lauf. / Wie hohles Holz zerbrechen sie die Tiere / und brauchen viele Völker brennend auf. / / Und ihre Menschen dienen in Kulturen / und fallen tief aus Gleichgewicht und Mass, / und nennen Fortschritt ihre Schneckenspuren / und fahren rascher, wo sie langsam fuhren, / und fühlen sich und funkeln wie die Huren / und lärmen lauter mit Metall und Glas. / / Es ist, als ob ein Trug sie täglich äffte, / sie können gar nicht mehr sie selber sein; / das Geld wächst an, hat alle ihre Kräfte / und ist wie Ostwind gross, und sie sind klein / und ausgeholt und warten, dass der Wein / und alles Gift der Tier- und Menschensäfte / sie reize zu vergänglichem Geschäfte.

The cities only want what they want
and tear up all in their path.
They break up animals like hollow wood
and consume the nations in the flames.

And their people are slaves to a culture
that deems their snail tracks progress;
falling deeply out of balance and measure,
they plunge ahead, where they used to go slow
- metal and glass loudly screeching -
with the sentiments and glare of whores.

It is as if they daily ape an illusion,
for they can no longer be themselves;
the power of gold, great as the east wind,
grows at their expense and makes them small,
holds them at bay, until the wine
and all the poisons of animals and humanity
tempt them into idle pursuits.

Die Städte aber wollen nur das Ihre
und reissen alles mit in ihren Lauf.
Wie hohles Holz zerbrechen sie die Tiere
und brauchen viele Völker brennend auf.

Und ihre Menschen dienen in Kulturen
und fallen tief aus Gleichgewicht und Mass,
und nennen Fortschritt ihre Schneckenspuren
und fahren rascher, wo sie langsam fuhren,
und fühlen sich und funkeln wie die Huren
und lärmen lauter mit Metall und Glas.

Es ist, als ob ein Trug sie täglich äffte,
sie können gar nicht mehr sie selber sein;
das Geld wächst an, hat alle ihre Kräfte
und ist wie Ostwind gross, und sie sind klein
und ausgeholt und warten, dass der Wein
und alles Gift der Tier- und Menschensäfte
sie reize zu vergänglichem Geschäfte.

Auguste Rodin, "The Crouching Woman"

And your poor suffer from these
and are burdened by all that they see;
fevered in a crisis of fire and ice,
they are pushed out to the street,
like strangers who die in the night;
and they are spat upon and covered in filth,
like things rotting under the sun;
and are assaulted at every turn –
by the cries of painted prostitutes,
the street lanterns' piercing light
and the blaring horns of cars.

If there be a voice for their protection –
so move it to be mindful and speak.

Und deine Armen leiden unter diesen
und sind von allem, was sie schauen, schwer
und glühen frierend wie in Fieberkrisen
und gehn, aus jeder Wohnung ausgewiesen,
wie fremde Tote in der Nacht umher;
und sind beladen mit dem ganzen Schmutze,
und wie in Sonne Faulendes bespien, –
von jedem Zufall, von der Dirnen Putze,
von Wagen und Laternen angeschrien.

Und gibt es einen Mund zu ihrem Schutze,
so mach ihn mündig und bewege ihn.

Master of Isabella di Chiaromonte,
"God's Minstrel St. Francis of Assisi",
Leaf from Book of Hours
(Naples, Italy 15th century)

SUFFRAGES
(MEMORIALS OF THE SAINTS)

Eugene Burnand, "Saint Francis of Assisi"
[Patron Saint of Animals and Nature]

O where is he, the one who left
possessions and time behind,
stood naked in the marketplace
before the bishop in his finery,
yet was clothed in the power of poverty;
the one most tender and loving of all,
the nightingales' brown-robed brother,
his life - like a young new year -
was full of pleasing wonder,
an enchantment on earth.

For he was not one of the always-tired,
who bit by bit become joyless;
walking the borders of the meadows,
he spoke alike to
small flowers and little brothers;
he talked of himself
and how he changed,
so that all was a joy to him;
his heart's lightness knew no end,
and not even the least
was overlooked.

He came out of light
to an even deeper light,
and had his history, his childhood;
matured like a girl to a woman,
smiles radiating from his face
and amusement in his way.

And when he sang, yesterday returned
with the long-forgotten in hand;
the nests in the trees went silent;
and only the sisters' hearts cried out,
because he touched them like a groom.

But then the pollen of his song
was released softly from his red mouth,
drifted dreamily to those in love

O wo ist der, der aus Besitz und Zeit
zu seiner grossen Armut so erstarkte,
dass er die Kleider abtat auf dem Markte
und bar einherging vor des Bischofs Kleid.
Der Innigste und Liebendste von allen,
der kam und lebte wie ein junges Jahr;
der braune Bruder deiner Nachtigallen,
in dem ein Wundern und ein Wohlgefallen
und ein Entzücken an der Erde war.

Denn er war keiner von den immer Müdern,
die freudeloser werden nach und nach,
mit kleinen Blumen wie mit kleinen Brüdern
ging er den Wiesenrand entlang und sprach.
Und sprach von sich und wie er sich verwende
so dass es allem eine Freude sei;
und seines hellen Herzens war kein Ende,
und kein Geringes ging daran vorbei.
Er kam aus Licht zu immer tieferm Lichte,
und seine Zelle stand in Heiterkeit.
Das Lächeln wuchs auf seinem Angesichte
und hatte seine Kindheit und Geschichte
und wurde reif wie eine Mädchenzeit.

Und wenn er sang, so kehrte selbst das Gestern
und das Vergessene zurück und kam;
und eine Stille wurde in den Nestern,
und nur die Herzen schrieen in den Schwestern,
die er berührte wie ein Bräutigam.

Dann aber lösten seines Liedes Pollen
sich leise los aus seinem roten Mund
und trieben träumend zu den Liebevollen
und fielen in die offenen Corollen
und sanken langsam auf den Blütengrund.

(continued on next page)

Eugene Burnand, "Saint Francis and Friar Masseo at the Fountain; Saint Francis Praises Poverty"[126]

settled on the open corollas and sank slowly onto the flowered ground. And they received him, the flawless one, into their body- their soul. And their eyes closed like roses, their hair like full nights of love. And both great and humble received him. Cherubs visited many animals to say, that their females would be fruitful, were like beautiful butterflies: for all things knew him and drew vitality from him. He lay on the ground and sang as he died, as simply as one unknown; his body and seed dissolved in song into the streams and trees and peacefully from the flowers looked down upon him. And when the sisters came, they cried over their beloved.	Und sie empfingen ihn, den Makellosen, in ihrem Leib, der ihre Seele war. Und ihre Augen schlossen sich wie Rosen, und voller Liebesnächte war ihr Haar. Und ihn empfing das Grosse und Geringe. Zu vielen Tieren kamen Cherubim, zu sagen, dass ihr Weibchen Früchte bringe, – und waren wunderschöne Schmetterlinge: denn ihn erkannten alle Dinge und hatten Fruchtbarkeit aus ihm. Und als er starb, so leicht wie ohne Namen, da war er ausgeteilt: sein Samen rann in Bächen, in den Bäumen sang sein Samen und sah ihn ruhig aus den Blumen an. Er lag und sang. Und als die Schwestern kamen, da weinten sie um ihren lieben Mann.

Eugene Burnand, "Saint Francis Preaches to the Birds"

I want to laud him. My praise – sweet as wine but not intoxicating – should win hearts and minds; my blood should pound, louder than the ocean, my cries going before me as the horns before an advancing army. And on Spring nights, gentle as April in the north, arriving late and anxious over every leaf, so will my stringed play blossom in the nearly empty camp. For my voice grows two-fold and is both fragrance and cry: the cry prepares the path ahead the fragrance must be angel, face and bliss to my isolation.	Ich will ihn preisen. Wie vor einem Heere die Hörner gehen, will ich gehn und schrein. Mein Blut soll lauter rauschen denn die Meere, mein Wort soll süss sein, dass man sein begehre, und doch nicht irremachen wie der Wein. Und in den Frühlingsnächten, wenn nicht viele geblieben sind um meine Lagerstatt, dann will ich blühn in meinem Saitenspiele so leise wie die nördlichen Aprile, die spät und ängstlich sind um jedes Blatt. Denn meine Stimme wuchs nach zweien Seiten und ist ein Duften worden und ein Schrein: die eine will den Fernen vorbereiten, die andere muss meiner Einsamkeiten Gesicht und Seligkeit und Engel sein.

Vincent van Gogh, "Saint-Rémy: Road with Cypress and Star"

O where is he –
 clear and ringing, feeling youthful joy –
 the one for whom the poor wait,
 not from afar?
 	
 Does he not rise in the dusk –
       poverty's great evening star?
	O wo ist er, der Klare, hingeklungen?
	 Was fühlen ihn, den Jubelnden und Jungen,
	 die Armen, welche harren, nicht von fern?
	
	 Was steigt er nicht in ihre Dämmerungen –
	       der Armut grosser Abendstern.

"…Nevertheless, I am perhaps already in the process of having begun my life: the life one does not give up on until one has completed it; and if one should die in the course of this honest work; then this life that one yet possessed as one's own descends on someone else, on a landscape or on God. If you have guided it up to a certain point it will complete itself at any cost – whether in your present time or later – so why be fearful?"

- Rainer Maria Rilke, The Schmargendorf Diary, 3 November 1899[127]

"Now everyone had gone out onto the dark forecourt, whose border walls twined white and soft around the night. And suddenly – did the wind deceive me? – voices, soft, rising, not like voices at the onset – voices setting out, but like voices in the middle of a song that always is in progress, and that only to those who become very still inside will suddenly make itself perceptible, and I hear: 'Glory to God in the Highest…' And then I knew that this song, that was rising as if climbing many steps, is always present, and that it makes itself known to us if we view singing profiles in front of starry nights."

- Rainer Maria Rilke, The Worpswede Diary, 3 October 1900[128]

Zanino di Pietro, "God's Minstrel: Saint Francis of Assisi"
Leaf from a Book of Hours, (Italy, mid-15th century)

CREDITS

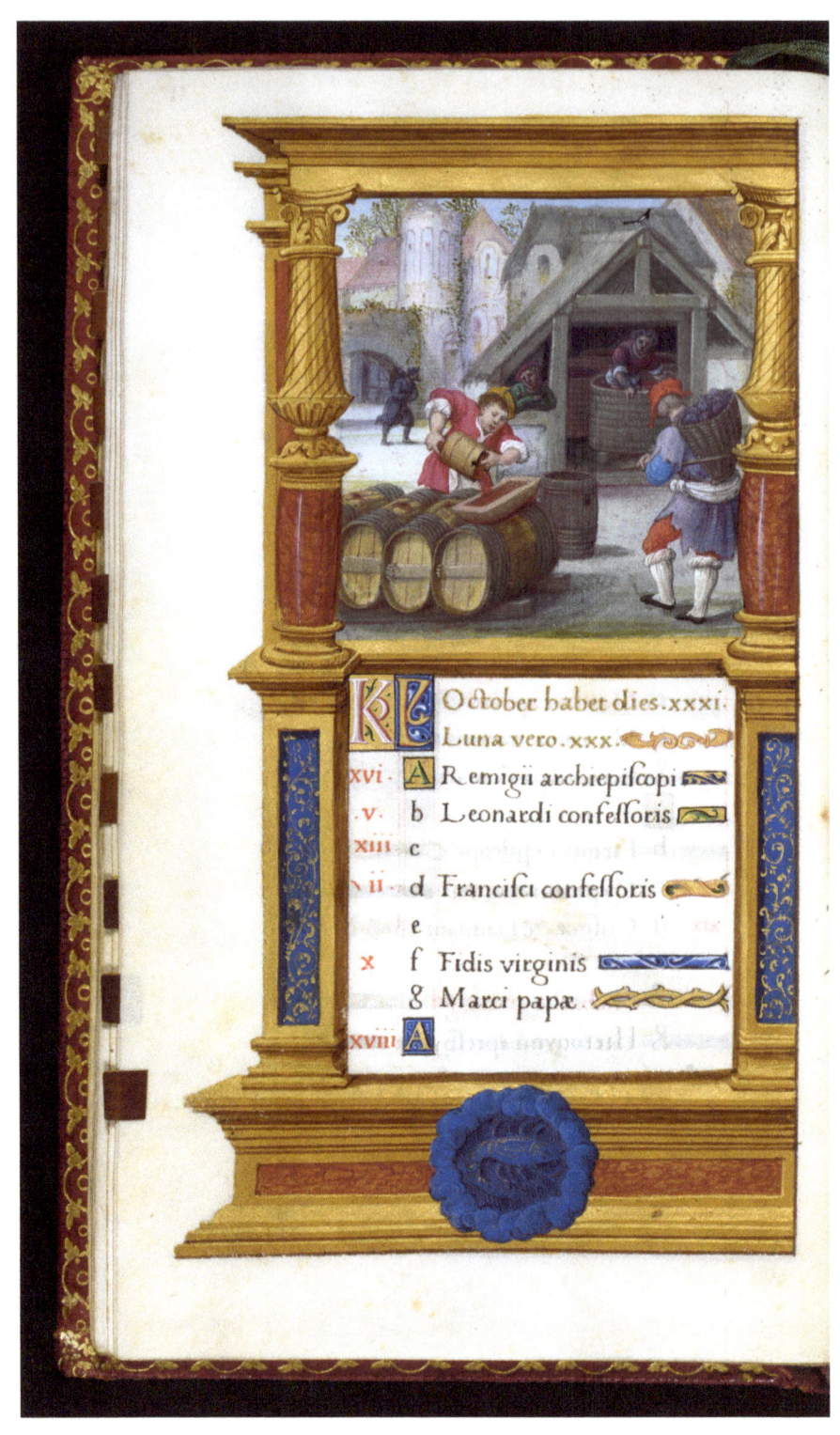

Master Jean de Mauléon,
Calendar Leaf for October from Book of Hours,
(France, ca. 1525)

Art Credits

Barlach, Ernst, "Death in Life", Photo by Rufus46 - Own work, CC BY-SA 3.0, https://commons.wikimedia.org/wiki/File:Ernst_Barlach_Tot_im_Leben_1926_Holz-1.jpg

Barlach, Ernst, "Hovering Angel", Photo by Jens Burkhardt-Plückhahn, CC-BY-SA 3.0, https://commons.wikimedia.org/wiki/File:Schwebender_Engel.jpg

Barlach, Ernst, "Reading Monks III", Photo by Wolfgang Sauber - Own work, CC BY-SA 4.0, https://commons.wikimedia.org/wiki/File:G%C3%BCstrow_Gertrudenkapelle_-_Barlachsammlung_Lesende_M%C3%B6nche.jpg

Barlach, Ernst, "Russian Beggar Woman", Photo by Jula2812 - Own work, CC BY-SA 4.0, https://commons.wikimedia.org/wiki/File:Russische_Bettlerin,_Bronze,_Ernst_Barlach.JPG

Barlach, Ernst, "The Abandoned Ones", Photo by Wolfgang Sauber – Own Work, CC BY - SA 4.0, https://commons.wikimedia.org/wiki/File:G%C3%BCstrow_Gertrudenkapelle_Barlachsammlung_Verlassene.jpg

Barlach, Ernst, "Sleeping Peasant Couple", Photo by Alter Jakob – Own Work, public domain dedication of photo, https://commons.wikimedia.org/wiki/File:Ernst_Barlach_Schlafende_Vagabunden_(Schlafendes_Bauernpaar)_1912.jpg

Barlach, Ernst, "The Ascetic", Photo by Rufus46 - Own Work, CC BY-SA 3.0, https://commons.wikimedia.org/wiki/File:Ernst_Barlach_Der_Asket_1925_Nussbaum-1.jpg

Barlach, Ernst, "The Blind Beggar", Photo by Vitold Muratov – Own Work, public domain dedication of photo, https://commons.wikimedia.org/wiki/File:%D0%A1%D0%BB%D0%B5%D0%BF%D0%BE%D0%B9_%D0%BD%D0%B8%D1%89%D0%B8%D0%B9.jpg

Barlach, Ernst, "The Desert Preacher", Photo by Rufus46 - Own Work, CC BY-SA 3.0, https://commons.wikimedia.org/wiki/File:Ernst_Barlach_Der_W%C3%BCstenprediger_1912_Eichenholz-1.jpg

Barlach, Ernst, "The First Day", Digital Image Courtesy of the Los Angeles County Museum of Art, www.lacma.org; https://collections.lacma.org/node/180454

Barlach, Ernst, "Wanderers", Photo by Daderot - Own Work, CC0 1.0 Universal Public Domain, "The museum permitted photography of this artwork without restriction"; Dedication,https://commons.wikimedia.org/wiki/File:Wanderers_by_Ernst_Barlach,_1913_walnut_-_Busch-Reisinger_Museum_-_DSC02382.JPG

Unknown Artist, "Leaf from a Book of Hours:
Lauds from the Hours of the Virgin,
Initial L with Christ Enthroned Holding a Globe",
(Ghent Belgium ca. early 14th century)

Barlach, Ernst, "Woman in the Wind", Photo by Richard Peter, Own Work, Deutsche Fotothek, CC BY-SA 3.0 de, https://commons.wikimedia.org/w/index.php?curid=7938617

Bartholdi, Frédéric Auguste, "Funerary Genius", Digital Image Courtesy of the Los Angeles County Museum of Art, www.lacma.org; https://collections.lacma.org/node/246537

Benini, Mauro, "Judas Holding a Rope and a Sack of Gold", Digital Image Courtesy of the Los Angeles County Museum of Art, www.lacma.org; https://collections.lacma.org/node/170213

Birago, Giovan Pietro, "Initial D with David in Prayer," Digital Image Courtesy of The Walters Art Museum, CC0 Universal Public Domain Dedication; http://art.thewalters.org/detail/21404/initial-d-with-david-in-prayer-2/

Blake, William, "Job's Tormentors", Digital Image in the Public Domain

Böcklin, Arnold, "Isle of the Dead", Digital Image in the Public Domain

Böcklin, Arnold, "Spring in a Narrow Gorge", Digital Image Courtesy of The J. Paul Getty Museum (Open Content Program); http://www.getty.edu/art/collection/objects/250519/arnold-bocklin-quell-in-einer-felsschlucht-spring-in-a-narrow-gorge-german-1881/

Book of Hours (Bruges, Belgium ca. 1460) and signed "Livinus Stuaert", Digital Image Courtesy of The Walters Art Museum, CC0 Universal Public Domain Dedication; http://art.thewalters.org/detail/15497/book-of-hours-34/

Book of Hours (Bruges, Belgium ca. 1460) with "IHS" embossed on binding, Digital Image Courtesy of The Walters Art Museum, CC0 Universal Public Domain Dedication; http://art.thewalters.org/detail/27297/book-of-hours-29/

Book of Hours created by the Masters of the Gold Scrolls for a patron devoted to Saint Francis (Bruges, Belgium ca. 1440-1450), Digital Image Courtesy of The Walters Art Museum, CC0 Universal Public Domain Dedication; http://art.thewalters.org/detail/9172/book-of-hours-27/

Book of Hours created by the circle of Willem Vrelant (Bruges, Belgium ca. 1460-1470), with ivory Christ on the binding, Digital Image Courtesy of The Walters Art Museum, CC0 Universal Public Domain Dedication; http://art.thewalters.org/detail/11347/book-of-hours-42/

Book of Hours created for an English patron by the workshop of Willem Vrelant

Unknown Artist, "Leaf from the Ruskin Book of Hours"
(Northeastern France, ca. 1300)

(Ghent-Bruges, Belgium, ca. 1460-1470), Digital Image Courtesy of The Walters Art Museum, CC0 Universal Public Domain Dedication; http://art.thewalters.org/detail/2983

Book of Hours created for a member of the Catalonian Almogàver family (Spain ca. 1510-1520), Digital Image Courtesy of The Walters Art Museum, CC0 Universal Public Domain Dedication; http://art.thewalters.org/detail/40777/almugavar-hours-2/

Book of Hours created for a member of the Augustinian Collegiate Church of Saint-Pierre (Lille, France 13th c.) with ivory carving on binding, Digital Image Courtesy of The Walters Art Museum, CC0 Universal Public Domain Dedication; http://art.thewalters.org/detail/3661/book-of-hours-20/

Book of Hours created for Philip I ("Philip the Fair"), Digital Image Courtesy of The Walters Art Museum, CC0 Universal Public Domain Dedication http://manuscripts.thewalters.org/viewer.php?id=W.440#page/1/mode/2up

Book of Hours (Ghent, Belgium ca. 1320-1330), Text in Latin, Flemish and French; Digital Image Courtesy of The Walters Art Museum, CC0 Universal Public Domain Dedication; http://art.thewalters.org/detail/14383/book-of-hours-24/

Book of Hours in Dutch (Haarlem, Netherlands 15th century), Digital Image Courtesy of The Walters Art Museum, CC0 Universal Public Domain Dedication; http://art.thewalters.org/detail/91288/binding-from-book-of-hours-in-dutch-3/

Book of Hours in Dutch created by the "Sarijs group" of the Brethren of the Common Life (Zwolle, Netherlands, ca. 1470), Digital Image Courtesy of The Walters Art Museum, CC0 Universal Public Domain Dedication; http://art.thewalters.org/detail/33460/book-of-hours-in-dutch-2/

Book of Hours in the style of the Master of the Prayerbook (Bruges, Belgium ca. 1500), Digital Image Courtesy of The Walters Art Museum, CC0 Universal Public Domain Dedication; http://art.thewalters.org/detail/14563/book-of-hours-37/

Book of Hours possibly created for the marriage of Louis I of Châtillon and Jeanne of Hainaut (France, 14th c.), Digital Image Courtesy of The Walters Art Museum, CC0 Universal Public Domain Dedication; http://art.thewalters.org/detail/24116/book-of-hours-8/

Book of Hours "treasure binding" with Adoration of the Magi on the front cover (Paris, France 19th century), Digital Image Courtesy of The Walters Art Museum, CC0 Universal Public Domain Dedication; http://art.thewalters.org/detail/9820/binding-for-a-book-of-hours/

Master of Edward IV (Style of), "Leaf from Book of Hours: Hours of the Virgin, Monks Playing Blind Man's Bluff", (Ghent, Belgium, ca. 1479)

Book of Hours (Use of Reims) (Northern France 15th century), Scribe identified as Paulinus de Sorcy, Digital Image Courtesy of University of Houston; https://digital.lib.uh.edu/collection/reims/item/437

Book of Hours (Use of Reims) (Northeastern France ca. 1450-1475), Digital Image Courtesy of The Walters Art Museum, CC0 Universal Public Domain Dedication; http://art.thewalters.org/detail/24994/book-of-hours-2/

Book of Hours (Use of Rome) (Bruges, Belgium ca. 1460-1470), Digital Image Courtesy of The Walters Art Museum, CC0 Universal Public Domain Dedication; http://art.thewalters.org/detail/15352

Book of Hours (Use of Saint-Omer) (Northeastern France early 14th century), possibly created for a female owner, Digital Image Courtesy of The Walters Art Museum, CC0 Universal Public Domain Dedication; http://art.thewalters.org/detail/30467/book-of-hours-30/

Bosch, Hieronymus, "Death and the Miser", Digital Image Courtesy of the National Gallery of Washington Art (Open Access Program); https://www.nga.gov/collection/art-object-page.41645.html

Bosch, Hieronymus, "The Conjurer", Digital Image in the Public Domain

Burnand, Eugene, "Saint Francis and Friar Masseo at the Fountain; Saint Francis Praises Poverty", from Thomas Okey, Little Flowers of Saint Francis (J.M. Dent & Sons Limited 1919); Digital Image in the Public Domain

Burnand, Eugene, "Saint Francis of Assisi", from Thomas Okey, Little Flowers of Saint Francis (J.M. Dent & Sons Limited 1919); Digital Image in the Public Domain

Burnand, Eugene, "Saint Francis Preaches to the Birds", from Thomas Okey, Little Flowers of Saint Francis (J.M. Dent & Sons Limited 1919); Digital Image in the Public Domain

Burne-Jones, Edward et al. (Artist-Designers), Lucy Orrinsmith, painter, "Labours of the Months", Images Courtesy of William Morris Gallery, London Borough of Waltham Forest

Cézanne, Paul, "Sous-Bois", Digital Image Courtesy of the Los Angeles County Museum of Art, www.lacma.org; https://collections.lacma.org/node/172409

Daumier, Honoré-Victorin, "Fugitives" or "Emigrants", Digital Image Courtesy of the National Gallery of Art, Washington (Open Access Program); https://images.nga.gov/?service=asset&action=show_zoom_window_popup&language=en&asset=19093&location=grid&asset_list=19093&basket_item_id=undefined

Unknown Artist, "Leaf from a Book of Hours:
Terce from the Hours of the Virgin,
Initial E with Seated Woman Holding Book",
(Ghent, Belgium ca. early 14th century)

Di Pietro, Zanino, "God's Minstrel: Saint Francis of Assisi", Digital Image Courtesy of The Walters Art Museum, CC0 1.0 Universal Public Domain Dedication; http://art.thewalters.org/detail/35275/leaf-from-book-of-hours-57

Dürer, Albrecht, "Christ on the Mount of Olives"; Digital Image Courtesy of the National Gallery of Art, Washington (Open Access Program); https://images.nga.gov/?service=asset&action=show_zoom_window_popup&language=en&asset=21585&location=grid&asset_list=154179,64050,137184,152661,136625,136628,116328,36655,91296,34166,86017,153037,36867,21884,47568,85974,23792,87904,91461,98506,21585,21047,86109,90969,20556&basket_item_id=undefined

Dürer, Albrecht, "Praying Hands"(study for an Apostle figure of the "Heller" altar); https://commons.wikimedia.org/wiki/File:Albrecht_D%C3%BCrer_Betende_H%C3%A4nde.jpg; also, digital image in the public domain

Gauguin, Paul, "Christmas Night (The Blessing of the Oxen)", Courtesy of Indianapolis Museum of Art at Newfields (public domain image); http://collection.imamuseum.org/artwork/82257/

Ghiberti, Lorenzo, 'Detail of Panel from the Gates of Paradise", Wjarek/ Adobe Stock

Günther, Matthäus, "Saint Luke Painting the Virgin Mary", Saint Peter and Paul Church in Mittenwald, Germany, Photo by GFreihalter - Own Work, CC0 3.0 – SA, https://commons.wikimedia.org/wiki/File:Mittenwald_St._Peter_und_Paul_Lukas_299.jpg

Ivanov, Alexander, "The Last Supper", Digital Image in the Public Domain

Kollwitz, Käthe, "In God's Hands", from Käthe Kollwitz, <u>Ich will wirken in dieser Zeit</u>, Introduction by Friedrich Ahlers-Hestermann (Verlag Gebr. Mann 1952); Digital Image in the Public Domain

Kollwitz, Käthe, "Praying Woman", from Arthur Bonus (ed.), <u>Das Käthe Kollwitz-Werk</u>, (Dresden: Carl Reissner Verlag 1930); Digital Image in the Public Domain

Kollwitz, Käthe, "Welcoming Death", from <u>Käthe Kollwitz</u>, Introduction by Carl Zigrosser (George Braziller 1951); Digital Image in the Public Domain

Kramskoy, Ivan, "Christ in the Wilderness", Digital Image in the Public Domain

Lalique, Rene, "Grande Ovale Joueuse de Flute", Setsuna75 / Adobe Stock

Manet, Édouard, "The Head of Christ", Digital Image in the Public Domain

Master of Guillebert de Mets, Master of the Lee Hours
and Master of Wauquelin's Alexander,
"Saint George and the Dragon",
Book of Hours (Ghent, Belgium ca. 1450–1455)

Master Jean de Mauléon, "Calendar Leaf of October from Book of Hours", (France ca. 1525), Digital Image Courtesy of The Walters Art Museum, CC0 1.0 Universal Public Domain Dedication; http://art.thewalters.org/detail/77734/leaf-from-book-of-hours-45/

Master of Edward IV (Style of), "Leaf from Book of Hours: Hours of the Virgin, Monks Playing Blind Man's Bluff", (Ghent, Belgium, ca. 1479), Digital Image Courtesy of The Walters Art Museum, CC0 1.0 Universal Public Domain Dedication; http://art.thewalters.org/detail/81321/monks-playing-blind-mans-bluff/

Master of Guillebert de Mets, Master of the Lee Hours and Master of Wauquelin's Alexander, "Saint George and the Dragon", Book of Hours (Ghent, Belgium ca. 1450-1455), Digital Image Courtesy of The J. Paul Getty Museum (Open Content Program), http://www.getty.edu/art/collection/objects/1449/master-of-guillebert-de-mets-and-master-of-the-lee-hours-and-master-of-wauquelin's-alexander-book-of-hours-flemish-about-1450-1455/

Master of Isabella di Chiaromonte, "Leaf from Book of Hours: God's Minstrel St. Francis of Assisi" (Italy, 15th c.), Digital Image Courtesy of The Walters Art Museum, CC0 1.0 Universal Public Domain Dedication; http://art.thewalters.org/detail/35855/leaf-from-book-of-hours-49/

Master of the Chronique scandaleuse, "Denise Poncher before a Vision of Death", Poncher Hours (Paris, France ca. 1500), Digital Image Courtesy of The J. Paul Getty Museum (Open Content Program), http://www.getty.edu/art/collection/objects/255124/master-of-the-chronique-scandaleuse-denise-poncher-before-a-vision-of-death-french-about-1500/

Master of the Harvard Hannibal, "Leaf from Book of Hours" (Paris, France ca. 1420-1430); Digital Image Courtesy of The J. Paul Getty Museum (Open Content Program), http://www.getty.edu/art/collection/objects/1486/master-of-the-harvard-hannibal-workshop-of-master-of-the-harvard-hannibal-book-of-hours-french-about-1420-1430/

Master of Walters, "Leaf from Barbavara Book of Hours" (Milan, Italy ca. 1440), Digital Image Courtesy of The Walters Art Museum, CC0 Universal Public Domain Dedication; http://art.thewalters.org/detail/39267/leaf-from-barbavara-book-of-hours-2/

Master of Walters, "Detail from a Leaf of the Barbavara Book of Hours" (Milan, Italy ca. 1440), Digital Image Courtesy of The Walters Art Museum, CC0 Universal Public Domain Dedication; https://art.thewalters.org/detail/29397/leaf-from-barbavara-book-of-hours-5/

Meunier, Constantin-Emile, "The Soil", Digital Image Courtesy of the Los Angeles County Museum of Art, www.lacma.org; https://collections.lacma.org/node/247288

Unknown Artist, "Leaf from a Book of Hours: None from the Hours of the Virgin, Initial F with Samson Wrestling a Lion", (Ghent, Belgium ca. early 14th century)

Millet, Jean-François, "Shepherdess and Her Flock", Digital Image Courtesy of The J. Paul Getty Museum (Open Content Program); http://www.getty.edu/art/collection/objects/26/jean-francois-millet-shepherdess-and-her-flock-french-1862-1863/

Modersohn, Otto, "On the Bank of the Moor", Digital Image in the Public Domain

Modersohn-Becker, Paula, "Clara Westhoff Rilke", Digital Image in the Public Domain

Monet, Claude, "Rouen Cathedral, West Façade, Sunlight", Digital Image Courtesy of the National Gallery of Art, Washington (Open Access Program); https://images.nga.gov/?service=asset&action=show_zoom_window_popup&language=en&asset=149357&location=grid&asset_list=149347,149357,148719&basket_item_id=undefined

Monnot, Pierre-Etienne, "Virgin Mary Swooning Over the Dead Body of Christ at the Foot of the Cross", Digital Image Courtesy of the National Gallery of Art, Washington (Open Access Program); https://images.nga.gov/?service=asset&action=show_zoom_window_popup&language=en&asset=150518&location=grid&asset_list=150518&basket_item_id=undefined

Morris, William, "Wandle", in Aymer Valence, <u>The Art of William Morris</u> (George Bell & Sons 1897), pg. 284; Photo by Mrsgamp –Own Work / CCA- BY- SA 3.0 License, https://commons.wikimedia.org/wiki/File:Artofwilliammorr00vall_0287.jpg; also https://archive.org/stream/artofwilliammorr00vall#page/n247/mode/2up

Morris, William, "Acanthus", Digital Image in the Public Domain

Morris, William, "Wild Tulips", Digital Image Courtesy of the Metropolitan Museum of Art, CC0 1.0 Universal Public Domain Dedication; Wikimedia Commons URL: https://commons.wikimedia.org/wiki/File:Wild_Tulip_MET_DP146520.jpg

Orlik, Emil, "Bohemian Village", Digital Image Courtesy of the Darrel C. Karl Collection

Orlik, Emil, "Figure Under Willow Tree", Digital Image Courtesy of the Darrel C. Karl Collection

Orlik, Emil, "Woman Gathering Wood in the Forest", Emil Heilbut (ed.), <u>Kunst und Künstler: Illustrierte Monatsschrift für Bildende Kunst und Kunstgewerbe</u> (1904); Digital Image Courtesy of the Eric van den Ing Collection, Saru Gallery, www.sarugallery.com

Pasternak, Leonid, "Rainer Maria Rilke in Moscow", Digital Image in the Public Domain

Redon, Odilon, "Cain and Abel", Digital Image Courtesy of the National Gallery of Art, Washington (Open Access Program);

Unknown Artist, "Leaf from Book of Hours:
Seven Penitential Psalms,
Initial D with the Martyrdom of the Apostle Peter",
(Ghent, Belgium ca. early 14th century)

https://images.nga.gov/?service=asset&action=show_zoom_window_popup&language=en&asset=153499&location=grid&asset_list=153499&basket_item_id=undefined

Rodin, Auguste, "Eternal Spring", Digital Image Courtesy of the Los Angeles County Museum of Art, www.lacma.org; https://collections.lacma.org/node/731623

Rodin, Auguste, "Head of a Girl", Digital Image Courtesy of the Los Angeles County Museum of Art, www.lacma.org; https://collections.lacma.org/node/176205

Rodin, Auguste, "La Douleur (de la Porte)", Digital Image Courtesy of the Los Angeles County Museum of Art, www.lacma.org; https://collections.lacma.org/node/183942

Rodin, Auguste, "Prodigal Son" or "Prayer", Digital Image Courtesy of the Los Angeles County Museum of Art, www.lacma.org; https://collections.lacma.org/node/240404

Rodin, Auguste, "St. John the Baptist", 2 Digital Images Courtesy of the Los Angeles County Museum of Art, www.lacma.org; https://collections.lacma.org/node/240591

Rodin, Auguste, "Large Clenched Hand", Digital Image Courtesy of the Los Angeles County Museum of Art (permission in writing)

Rodin, Auguste, "Memorial Relief (Hand of a Child)", Digital Image Courtesy of the National Gallery of Art, Washington (Open Access Program); https://images.nga.gov/?service=asset&action=show_zoom_window_popup&language=en&asset=57200&location=grid&asset_list=57200&basket_item_id=undefined

Rodin, Auguste, "The Age of Bronze", Photo by Museo Soumaya, CC-BY-SA 4.0, https://commons.wikimedia.org/wiki/File:La_edad_de_bronce.jpg

Rodin, Auguste, "The Crouching Woman", Digital Image Courtesy of the Los Angeles County Museum of Art, www.lacma.org; https://collections.lacma.org/node/171940

Rodin, Auguste, "The Cry", Digital Image Courtesy of the Los Angeles County Museum of Art; www.lacma.org; https://collections.lacma.org/node/240405

Rodin, Auguste, "The Hand of God", Xlopchik / 3dSky.org

Rodin, Auguste, "The Storm", Photo by Captainm – Own Work, CCA- BY- SA 3.0 License, https://commons.wikimedia.org/wiki/File:Rodin_-_La_Tempete.JPG

Saint, Lawrence, painting of a panel from the "Acts of Mercy" stained glass window in All Saints' Church, York, England, from H. Arnold, Stained Glass of the Middle Ages in England and France (Adam and Charles Black 1913), at page 200-201 (Plate XXXVII), Digital image in the public domain

Master of the Chronique scandaleuse,
"Denise Poncher before a Vision of Death",
Poncher Hours, Office of the Dead
(Paris, France ca. 1500)

Sanmartino, Giuseppe (Circle of), "Veiled Christ", Digital Image Courtesy of the Los Angeles County Museum of Art, www.lacma.org; https://collections.lacma.org/node/172385

Signature of Rainer Maria Rilke, Digital Image in the Public Domain

Steichen, Edward, "M. Auguste Rodin" (photograph), Brooklyn Museum Online Collection, Digital Image in the Public Domain; https://www.brooklynmuseum.org/opencollection/objects/166548

Strozzi, Zanobi di Benedetto, "Leaf from Adimari Book of Hours" (Italy, 15th c.), Digital Image Courtesy of The Walters Art Museum, CC0 1.0 Universal Public Domain Dedication; http://art.thewalters.org/detail/1563/leaf-from-adimari-book-of-hours-12/

Taft, Lorado, "Solitude of the Soul", Digital Image Courtesy of the Los Angeles County Museum of Art, www.lacma.org; https://collections.lacma.org/node/176212

Tiemann, Walter, Artwork on the cover and first page of Rainer Maria Rilke's *Das Stunden-Buch*; Digital Image in the Public Domain and also included under the Doctrine of Fair Use.

Unknown Artist, "Leaf from a Book of Hours: Lauds from the Hours of the Virgin, Initial L with Christ Enthroned Holding a Globe", (Ghent Belgium ca. early 14th century), Digital Image Courtesy of The Walters Art Museum, CC0 1.0 Universal Public Domain Dedication; https://art.thewalters.org/detail/95315/leaf-from-book-of-hours-lauds-from-hours-of-the-virgin-initial-l-with-christ-enthroned-holding-globe/

Unknown Artist, "Leaf from a Book of Hours: Terce from the Hours of the Virgin, Initial E with Seated Woman Holding Book", (Ghent, Belgium ca. early 14th century), Digital Image Courtesy of The Walters Art Museum, CC0 1.0 Universal Public Domain Dedication; https://art.thewalters.org/detail/95318/leaf-from-book-of-hours-terce-from-hours-of-the-virgin-initial-e-with-seated-woman-holding-book/

Unknown Artist, "Leaf from a Book of Hours: None from the Hours of the Virgin, Initial F with Samson Wrestling a Lion", (Ghent, Belgium ca. early 14th century), Digital Image Courtesy of The Walters Art Museum, CC0 1.0 Universal Public Domain Dedication; https://art.thewalters.org/detail/95325/leaf-from-book-of-hours-none-from-hours-of-the-virgin-initial-f-with-samson-wrestling-a-lion/

Unknown Artist, "Leaf from Book of Hours: Seven Penitential Psalms, Initial D with the Martyrdom of the Apostle Peter", (Ghent, Belgium ca. early 14th century); Digital Image Courtesy of The Walters Art Museum, CC0 1.0 Universal Public Domain Dedication; http://art.thewalters.org/detail/95335/leaf-from-book-of-hours-seven-penitential-psalms-initial-d-with-the-martyrdom-of-the-apostle-peter/

Unknown Artist, "Leaf from a Book of Hours:
Vespers from Hours of the Virgin:
Initial D with the Anointing of Christ's Body before Entombment",
(Ghent, Belgium ca. early 14th century)

Unknown Artist, "Leaf from a Book of Hours: Vespers from Hours of the Virgin: Initial D with the Anointing of Christ's Body Before Entombment", (Ghent, Belgium ca. early 14th century), Digital Image Courtesy of The Walters Art Museum, CC0 1.0 Universal Public Domain Dedication; https://art.thewalters.org/detail/95326/leaf-from-book-of-hours-vespers-from-hours-of-the-virgin-initial-d-with-the-anointing-of-christs-body-before-entombment/

Unknown Artist, "Leaf from the Ruskin Book of Hours" (Northeastern France, ca. 1300); Digital Image Courtesy of The J. Paul Getty Museum (Open Content Program), http://www.getty.edu/art/collection/objects/1387/unknown-maker-ruskin-hours-french-about-1300/

Unknown Artist, "Leaf from Litany in a Book of Hours: Three Clerics Singing before a Lectern (France, ca. 1300-1325); Digital Image Courtesy of The Walters Art Museum, CC0 1.0 Universal Public Domain Dedication; https://art.thewalters.org/detail/20096/three-clerics-singing-before-a-lectern-2/

Unknown Artist, "May Calendar: Falconer Riding a Horse", Leaf from a Book of Hours (Lille, France, 13th c.), Digital Image Courtesy of The Walters Art Museum, CC0 1.0 Universal Public Domain Dedication; http://art.thewalters.org/detail/94532/leaf-from-book-of-hours-may-calendar-falconer-riding-a-horse/

Unknown Artist, Russian Ikon (19th c.), "Descent into Hell", Digital Image Courtesy of The Walters Art Museum, CC0 1.0 Universal Public Domain Dedication; http://art.thewalters.org/detail/2681/icon-of-the-descent-into-hell/

Unknown Artist, "Dreamer Sculpture", Chartres Cathedral, Photo by Richard Nilsen, Own Work, Digital Image courtesy of Richard Nilsen

Unknown Artist, "Dog Chasing Hare", Marginalia from Leaf of Office of the Dead, French Book of Hours 14th c.,The Walters Museum CC0 1.0 Universal Public Domain Dedication; http://art.thewalters.org/detail/4059/a-funeral-service-2/

Unknown Artist, "Risen Christ" (Italy, Florence ca. 1620), Digital Image Courtesy of the Los Angeles County Museum of Art, www.lacma.org; https://collections.lacma.org/node/242416

Unknown Artist, "Crucifixion Icon" (Russia ca. 16th Century), Digital Image Courtesy of The Walters Art Museum, CC0 1.0 Universal Public Domain Dedication; http://art.thewalters.org/detail/40760/crucifixion-16/

Master of the Harvard Hannibal,
"Leaf from Book of Hours"
[Resurrection of the Dead]
(Paris, France, ca. 1415 – 1430)

Unknown Artist, Detail of Leaf from an Antiphonary (Venice, Italy, ca. 1505), Digital Image Courtesy of The Walters Art Museum, CC0 Universal Public Domain Dedication; http://art.thewalters.org/detail/1515/antiphonarium-2/

Unknown Artist, "The Dove (Holy Spirit) in Stained Glass", Howgill/Adobe Stock

Unknown Photographer, Photo of Lou Andreas-Salomé ca. 1900, Digital Image in the Public Domain

Uspensky Sobor (Cathedral of the Assumption), Moscow, Russia: Photo by Jimmy Weee - Own Work, CC BY 2.0 Generic https://commons.wikimedia.org/wiki/File:Moscow_(8352327054).jpg

van Gogh, Vincent, "Saint-Rémy - Road with Cypress and Star", Digital Image in the Public Domain

van Gogh, Vincent, "Pine Trees Against a Red Sky with Setting Sun", Digital Image in the Public Domain

van Gogh, Vincent, "Landscape at St. Remy", Courtesy of Indianapolis Museum of Art at Newfields (public domain image); http://collection.imamuseum.org/artwork/56838/

van Rysselberghe, Théo, "Big Clouds", Courtesy of Indianapolis Museum of Art at Newfields (public domain image); http://collection.imamuseum.org/artwork/77448/

Venetian Clock, Javarman / Adobe Stock

Veneziano, Paolo, "St. John the Baptist (fragment)", Digital Image Courtesy of the Los Angeles County Museum of Art, www.lacma.org; https://collections.lacma.org/node/229292

Vienna Book of Hours, binding created by Abigail Quandt, The Walters Art Museum (1985), Digital Image Courtesy of The Walters Art Museum, CC0 Universal Public Domain Dedication; http://art.thewalters.org/detail/90562/binding-from-vienna-book-of-hours/

Vigeland, Gustav, "Gate of Youth and Column of Life", Nanismova / Adobe Stock

Vigeland, Gustav, "Gate of Youth", Nanismova / Adobe Stock

Vigeland, Gustav, "Mother and Child", Mundafora / Adobe Stock

Vigeland, Gustav, "Old Man", Nanismova / Adobe Stock

Vogeler, Heinrich, "Virgin Mary", Digital Image in the Public Domain

Vogeler, Heinrich, "Women in Mourning", Digital Image in the Public Domain

Unknown Artist, "Leaf from the Litany in a Book of Hours: Three Clerics Singing before a Lectern" (France, ca. 1300-1325) [note the traditional Litany ending of "orate pro nobis" – "Pray for us"]

Vogeler, Heinrich, "Sommerabend" ("Summer Evening"), Digital Image in the Public Domain

Vuillard, Édouard, "Une Gallerie au Gymnase", Digital Image Courtesy of the Indianapolis Museum of Art at Newfield's (public domain image); http://collection.imamuseum.org/artwork/69248/

Explanation of Creative Commons licenses (e.g., CC0 and CC by SA): https://en.wikipedia.org/wiki/Creative_Commons_license

Other Credits:

"Written", artwork image incorporated into front cover of The SelfScape Book of Hours for the Sixth Day of Creation, courtesy of Sandra Bowden, artist (www.sandrabowden.com)

Rose stained glass window in the Cathedral of Notre Dame, Paris, incorporated into front cover of The SelfScape Book of Hours for the Seventh Day of Creation, Scaligar/Adobe Stock

The German texts of the selected poems from Rainer Maria Rilke's *Das Stunden-Buch* quoted in this volume were based on an Insel-Verlag 1920 edition.

The Ex Libris image before the Table of Contents is an adaptation of Rainer Maria Rilke's Ex Libris label which bore the name "René Maria Rilke", since it pre-dated the change of his name from René to Rainer. The original Ex Libris label image is in the public domain and the modification made to it was to change the name on the label to "Rainer Maria Rilke".

Excerpts from The Holy Bible, Revised Standard Version (Second Catholic Edition) (Ignatius Press 2006), included with the permission of Ignatius Press:

- New Testament, copyright 1946
- Old Testament, Copyright 1952
- The Apocrypha, copyright 1957
- Revised Standard Version Bible, Catholic Edition, Copyright 1965, 1966, Division of Christian Education of the National Council of the Churches of Christ in the United States of America
- Revised Standard Version Bible, Ignatius Edition, Copyright 2006, Division of Christian Education of the National Council of the Churches of Christ in the United States of America

For more information on the "Labours of the Month" images, see http://www.wmgallery.org.uk/collection/browse-the-collection/the-labours-of-the-month-c216-1862/object-type/ceramics/page/2; Digital Images Courtesy of William Morris Gallery, London Borough of Waltham Forest

Book of Hours "Treasure Binding"
Created for the Paris Exposition Universelle in 1878
(Firm of Gruel & Engelmann and Jeweler Alexis Falize)

END NOTES

Book of Hours (Bruges, Belgium ca. 1460)
Original binding of boards covered with leather
and signed "Livinus Stuaert"

[1] "Sie zeigten mir die kleinen Abendblätter, und ich fühle, wie aus jedem Entwurf, aus schwarz und rot, mit mehr als Wirklichkeitentgegenwuchs; jenes Sein, das nur die tiefste Kunst in tiefen Stunden hinzustellen vermag, erfüllte sich in diesen Skizzen…Damals dachte ich: Einmal, möchte ich solche Stunden haben wie diese Blätter. Dunkel and doch überdeutlich, mit reichen, nicht zählbaren Dingen und Gestalten, die von schöner Geduld umflossen sind. Jetzt weiss ich, dass ich auf solche Stunden zu lebe, auf solche Gedichte zu." - Ruth Sieber-Rilke and Carl Sieber, Rainer Maria Rilke, Briefe aus den Jahren 1892 - 1904 (Insel-Verlag 1939), pp. 114-115.

[2] "[T]he *Book of Hours* has in recent years suffered from a kind of inferiority complex. Before the war, it was amongst Rilke's most popular works…Yet in the second half of the twentieth century, it has steadily been surpassed in popularity by the brilliance of its younger brothers the *New Poems*, the *Duino Elegies*, and the *Sonnets to Orpheus*…Whilst the lasting brilliance of Rilke's other major works is beyond question, this view of *The Book of Hours* as a slight embarrassment to its author needs urgent revising. There is a sense, indeed, in which it is not only Rilke's first major work, but also his defining work, at least in terms of his development: the subsequent *New Poems* react against it, the later *Duino Elegies* look back to it.", Susan Ranson (translator) and Ben Hutchinson (Editor), Rainer Maria Rilke's The Book of Hours: A New Translation with Commentary (Camden House 2008), pg. xii.

[3] See Rainer Maria Rilke Letter of July 19, 1915 to Elsa Bruckmann, Ruth Sieber-Rilke (ed.), Rainer Maria Rilke Briefe (Zweiter Band: 1914-1926) (Insel-Verlag 1950), pp. 27-29.

[4] Radio Wien Rilke Abend ("Rilke Evening on Radio Vienna") on December 20, 1925: Erika Wagner reading from Rilke's *Book of Hours*: http://anno.onb.ac.at/cgi-content/anno?aid=raw&datum=19251213&seite=28&zoom=33&query=%22rilke%22%2B%22stundenbuch%22&ref=anno-search.

[5] See, e.g., the December 30, 1926, front page obituary in the Vienna Reichspost: "Sein 'Stundenbuch' wird vielfach als sein bedeutsamstes Werk angesehen." ("His Book of Hours is widely regarded to be his most important work"), at http://anno.onb.ac.at/cgi-content/anno?aid=rpt&datum=19261230&query=%22rilke%22+%22stundenbuch%22&ref=anno-search.

[6] "Dem 'Buch der Bilder' liess Rilke ein Gedichtwerk mit dem Titel 'Das Stundenbuch' folgen. Dieses schöne and fromme *livre d'heures* gab der Inselverlag zu Leipzig in einem reizenden Gewande heraus: Es ist bei Drugulin auf seinem Van-Geldernpapier gedruckt und mitte in paar Zeichnungen von Walter Tiemann geschmückt. Das Andachtsbuch zerfällt in drei Abteilungen: "Vom mönschischen Leben", "Von der Pilgerschaft" und "Von der Armut und dem Tode". Wie rinnende Bäche in abendlichen Wiesenfluren sind diese Werke; sie scheinen keinen Anfang and kein Ende zu haben, es ist ein süsses, melodisches Raunen von den Geheimnissen, die Gott umgeben. Die Werke sind berührt von dem Flügelschlag wundervollen Sehertums; hier is eine stammelnde hingabe an das Göttliche; eine Demut und ein tiefer Glaube; eine ergreifende Lyrik, erfüllt von Bildern und Gesichten, die alle zu Gott führen.", Prager Tagblatt, No. 66 (1909), pp. 35-36.

[7] "Rilke is ein Christ von echt mittelalterlichem Schlage: einer, dem Gott alles und die Welt nichts als eine buntgemalte Hieroglyphe für seinen heiligen Namen ist, und dessen ganzes Leben nur ein sehnsüchtiges Tasten durch die Dinge hindurch zum Eigentlichen, Wesentlichen, höchsten ist….Aber wie man es nennen mag: in der Masse dieser Verse is das 'Stundenbuch' geoffen, dieser aufwühlende Gebetsstrom, diese tausendfältige Variation über den Namen Gottes, diese Lösung aller weltlichen Gestalt in Gott."- Julius Bab, "Das Evangelium Brigge", Die Schaubühne 6, No. 22-23 (2 June 1910), pp 583-584.

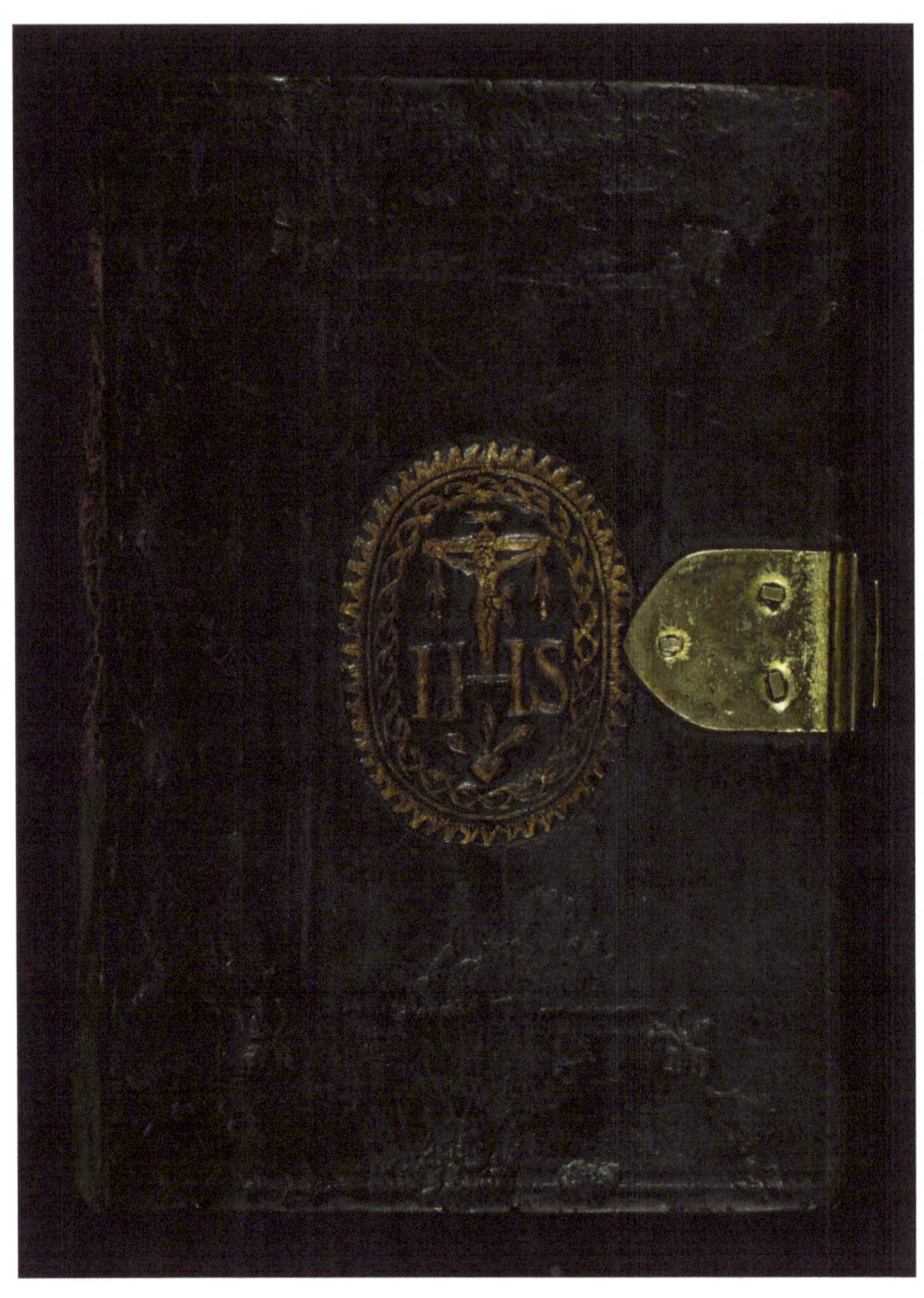

Book of Hours created by an artist in the circle of Willem Vrelant
(Bruges, Belgium ca. 1460)
Non-original binding of boards
covered by leather (Belgium, 17th century)

[8] See Rainer Maria Rilke letter to Clara Rilke, 22 February, 1906: "Und Morgen, und Nachmittage mit der Bibel auf dem Lesepult…" ("And morning and afternoons, with the Bible on the writing desk…"), Ruth Sieber-Rilke and Carl Sieber (ed.), Rainer Maria Rilke: Briefe aus den Jahren 1902-1906 (Insel-Verlag 1930), pg. 302; see also Rainer Maria Rilke letter to Franz Xaver Kappus, 5 April 1903, where Rilke advises that he views the Bible as indispensable and always has it by his side.

[9] See, e.g., *New Poems* (1907): Joshua's Farewell, Mount of Olives, Saint Sebastien, Departure of the Prodigal Son; *Neue Gedichte Anderer Teil* (1908): Saul among the Prophets, Samuel's Appearance to Saul, The Comforting of Elijah, Esther, Jeremiah, Magnificat, Crucifixion, The Risen One, The Reliquary, Judgment Day, From the Life of a Saint, The Stylite; *The Book of Images* (1902-1906): Annunciation: The Words of the Angel, Last Supper, The Guardian Angel, At the Cartusian Monastery; *The Life of the Virgin Mary* (1912); *Poems* (1902-1926): Assumption of Mary, The Raising of Lazarus, Christ's Descent into Hell, Emmaeus, Elegy of a Nun, Saint Christopher. For English translations, see Annemarie Kidder, Pictures of God: Rilke's Religious Poetry Including "The Life of the Virgin Mary" (First Page Publications 2005).

[10] Rainer Maria Rilke, "Christus: Elf Visionen", in Ernst Zinn (editor), Rainer Maria Rilke Sämtliche Werke in Zwölf Bänden, Band 5 (Insel-Verlag 1975), pp. 127-169; see also Annemarie Kidder, Pictures of God: Rilke's Religious Poetry Including "The Life of the Virgin Mary" (First Page Publications 2005), pp. xiii-xiv: "Apart from the intimate relationship with Lou that the Visions symbolized to Rilke and possibly made him postpone their publication, he may have also felt that his readership was not ready for a depiction of Christ that called into question traditional tenets of Christian dogma. For example, in Rilke's poetry, the Trinitarian concept of God as Father, Son, and Holy Spirit is missing. The doctrine of Christ's death and resurrection is reinterpreted on a personal, individualistic level, not in the context of the church as Christ's body. And Christ is more human than divine and does not have the exclusive substitutionary role as mediator between God and humanity that orthodox church doctrine would assign to him. Thus, Rilke's Christ emerges as a unique, perennial teacher who by his human compassion, suffering, and solitude invites and models a God-search driven by feeling and an ethics of love."

[11] See Rainer Maria Rilke letter to his publisher, Anton Kippenberg on January 8, 1912 ("Dreikönigstag"), "Ich glaube aber, dass ausser den *Christusvisionen* nichts Brauchbares dabei sich ergeben kann. Und diese grossen Gedichte, die ich so lange nicht wiedergesehen habe, müsste ich unbedingt eine Weile um mich haben und auf meinem Gewissen, bevor sie (fast fünfzehn Jahre nach ihrer Entstehung) mit den anderen alten Sachen unter die Leute kommen…" ("But I believe that apart from the *Visions of Christ*, nothing useful can be found. And these great poems, which I have not looked at for so long, I would absolutely need to keep with me for a while and on my conscience, before they are released to the public (almost fifteen years after their creation) along with the other old works.") - Ruth Sieber-Rilke und Carl Sieber (ed.), Rainer Maria Rilke: Briefe an seinen Verleger (Erster Band: 1906-1926) (Insel-Verlag 1949), pg. 159.

[12] "Erst muss man Gott irgendwo finden, ihn erfahren, also so unendlich, so überaus, so ungeheurer vorhanden –, dann sei's Furcht, sei's Staunen, sei's Atemlosigkeit, sei's am Ende – Liebe, was mann dann zu ihm fasst, darauf kommt es kaum noch an, - aber die Glaube, dieser Zwang zu Gott, hat keinen Platz, wo einer mit der Entdeckung Gottes begonnen hat, in der es dann kein Aufhören mehr gibt, mag man an welcher Stelle immer begonnen haben." - Ruth Sieber-Rilke (ed.), Rainer Maria Rilke: Briefe aus den Jahren 1914-1926 (Insel-Verlag Leipzig 1950), pg. 284.

[13] As they advise in the endnotes to their translation, "To avoid making Rilke sound too pious, we changed his 'frömmsten Gefühle' ('most devout feelings') to 'what waits within me'", Anita Barrows and Joanna Macy, Rilke's Book of Hours: Love Poems to God (Riverhead Books 2005), note I, 12, pg. 244.

Book of Hours created for a member of the Augustinian Collegiate Church of Saint-Pierre (Lille, France 13th century)
Non-original binding of calfskin bound between boards covered with brown morocco, ivory, silver, and gilding (Paris, France 19th century)

[14] The "Middle Ages" spanned from the 5th to the end of the 15th centuries and are usually broken down into three periods: the Early Middle Ages (5th century to 10th century), the High Middle Ages (1000 AD to 1250 AD) and the Late Middle Ages (1250 AD to 1500 AD) - https://en.wikipedia.org/wiki/High_Middle_Ages.

[15] "Diese letzte Woche bin ich jeden Tag von 10 Uhr an bis 5 Uhr nachmittags in der Nationalbibliothek gewesen und habe viele Bücher gelesen und viele Reproduktionen von Kathedralen aus dem XII. und XIII. Jahrhundert gesehen. Du, das war eine grosse, grosse Kunst. Je mehr man sich mit ihren Dingen befasst, desto tiefer fühlt man den Wert und die Köstlichkeit der Arbeit: denn diese Kathedralen, diese Berge und Gebirge des Mittelalters, wären nie fertig geworden, wenn sie aus Inspirationen hätten entstehen sollen. Da musste ein Tag wie der andere kommen und Hand anlegen, und wenn nicht jeder eine Inspiration war, so war doch jeder ein Weg dazu." - Ruth Sieber-Rilke and Carl Sieber (ed.), Rainer Maria Rilke: Briefe aus den Jahren 1892 - 1904 (Insel-Verlag 1939), pp. 269-270.

[16] John Harthan, The Book of Hours (Thomas Y. Crowell Company 1977), pg. 11.

[17] See https://en.wikipedia.org/wiki/Jean_Fouquet.

[18] "Wir haben gestern diesen Regen sich vorbereiten sehen draussen auf dem Land, in Buchengängen, über weiten Wiesen und Wasserflächen, in den Fenstern eines alten Schlosses: in Chantilly. Das war kein eigentlich königliches Schloss, und so ist es auch nicht. Es gehörte den Condés, und es ist anders, intimer als Saint-Cloud oder Versailles oder Saint-Germain …Drinnen eine in später Zeit verdorbene Pracht. Eine Reihe von Bildern…Miniaturen Fouquets (Heilige und Christuslegenden), aus dem livre d'heures des Étienne Chevalier genommen…" – Ruth Sieber-Rilke und Carl Sieber, Rainer Maria Rilke: Briefe aus den Jahren 1904 - 1907 (Insel-Verlag 1939), pp. 150-151; see also, https://en.wikipedia.org/wiki/Hours_of_%C3%89tienne_Chevalier.

[19] "Ich staune, staune dieses vierzehnte Jahrhundert an, das mir immer das merkwürdigste war, unserem so genau engegengesetzt… [diese] Welt, in die der Grosse Tod des Jahres 1348, berauscht von so viel Dasein, seiner selbst nicht mehr mächtig, hineinzielte." - Ruth Sieber-Rilke (ed.), Rainer Maria Rilke: Briefe aus den Jahren 1897 - 1914 (Insel-Verlag 1950), pg. 373.

[20] See, e.g., Ernst Zinn (editor), Rainer Maria Rilke Sämtliche Werke in Zwölf Bänden, Band 5 (Insel-Verlag 1975), pp. 354-355, 368; see also pg. 312, where the poem about Cain killing Abel has this annotation:" "Als der Mönch die Bibel las an einem stürmischen Abende, da fand der, dass vor allem Tode die Ermordung Abels geschah. Und er erschrak tief im Herzen…" ("As the monk read the Bible on a stormy night, he found that the murder of Abel by Cain occurred before all other murders. And he was deeply shocked in his heart.")

[21] Saints Cosmas and Damian were Christian physicians in late 14th- early 15th century Syria who tended to the poor without asking for any payment ("silverless" physicians or "anargyroi" in the original Greek); see https://en.wikipedia.org/wiki/Saints_Cosmas_and_Damian.

[22] See https://en.wikipedia.org/wiki/Breviary.

Ghent Associates, Philip I ("Philip the Fair") Book of Hours
(Ghent, Belgium 15th century)
Original binding of boards covered in leather

[23] See https://www.ecatholic2000.com/benedict/rule.shtml.

[24] See https://en.wikipedia.org/wiki/Matins.

[25] Dr. L.M.J. Delaissé, quoted in John Harthan, The Book of Hours (Thomas Y. Crowell Company 1977), pg. 9.

[26] https://en.wikipedia.org/wiki/Treasure_binding.

[27] Eamon Duffy, Marking the Hours: English People and Their Prayers 1240-1570 (Yale University Press 2006), pg. 15; see also, "The Abbé Leroquais established a basic classification of the contents of Books of Hours. Three elements are distinguished: essential, secondary and accessory texts. The essential texts are those extracted from the Breviary: the Calendar, the Little Office or Hours of the Virgin, the Penitential Psalms, the Litany, the Office of the Dead and the Suffrages of the Saints. Like the Breviary, the Book of Hours in turn attracted further texts which extended its devotional scope – as well as increasing the variety of its contents. These secondary texts comprise the Sequences, which are the passages from the four Gospels in which the Evangelists Matthew, Mark, Luke and John describe the coming of Christ; the account of the Passion given in the Gospel of St. John; two special prayers to the Virgin which enjoyed great popularity, the *Obsecro te* ("I implore thee") and *O Intemerata* ("O matchless one"); a number of shorter alternative Offices, the Hours of the Cross, of the Holy Spirit and (less often) of the Holy Trinity; the Fifteen Joys of the Virgin; and the Seven Requests of the Savior. Even this substantial addition was not enough to satisfy the yearning for devotion among the laity. It was increased by Leroquais' third element, the accessory texts. These comprise more extracts from the Psalter, and miscellaneous prayers. The Fifteen Gradual Psalms (also present in the Breviary in this form) and the Psalter of St. Jerome represent a further appropriation of the inexhaustible riches of Psalmody. The Gradual Psalms comprise numbers 119-33, the short and beautiful psalms sometimes considered to be those recited by Jewish pilgrims 'going up' (*gradus*, a step) to Jerusalem…The arrangement of a 'typical' Book of Hours is given below…

1. Calendar
2. Sequences of the Gospels
3. The prayer *Obsecro te*
4. The prayer *O Intemerata*
5. Hours of the Virgin
6. Hours of the Cross
7. Hours of the Holy Spirit
8. Penitential Psalms
9. Litany
10. Office of the Dead
11. Suffrages of the Saints"

- John Harthan, The Book of Hours (Thomas Y. Crowell Company 1977), pp. 14-15.

[28] "…First comes a Calendar, essential for making sure that the right devotions are performed on each day in the year; for the content of each service varies according to the season, the day of the week, the saints' days and other feasts, both fixed and moveable." - John Harthan, The Book of Hours (Thomas Y. Crowell Company 1977), pg. 12.

[29] John Harthan, The Book of Hours (Thomas Y. Crowell Company 1977), pg. 24.

Book of Hours created for an English patron
by the workshop of Willem Vrelant
(Ghent-Bruges, Belgium, ca. 1460-1470)
Original binding of boards covered by leather

[30] For an in-depth exploration of Golden Numbers, Dominical Letters, Simplex and Duplex Feasts and other intricacies of the calendars contained in a medieval Book of Hours, see Roger Wieck, The Medieval Calendar: Locating Time in the Middle Ages (The Morgan Library & Museum 2017).

[31] See https://en.wikipedia.org/wiki/Penitential_Psalms and https://en.wikipedia.org/wiki/Song_of_Ascents. (note that the psalms have different numbers in the Septuagint and the Vulgate versions of the Bible).

[32] See https://en.wikipedia.org/wiki/Gloria_Patri.

[33] See https://en.wikipedia.org/wiki/Antiphon.

[34] For a hypertext version of a medieval Book of Hours in both Latin and English, see http://medievalist.net/hourstxt/home.htm.

[35] Eamon Duffy, Marking the Hours: English People & Their Prayers 1240-1570 (Yale University Press 2006), pg. 29.

[36] For an illustrated tutorial on the medieval Book of Hours, see http://www.medievalbooksofhours.com/learn#advanced,

[37] John Harthan, The Book of Hours (Thomas Y. Crowell Company 1977), pg. 17.

[38] Psalms 6, 31, 37, 50, 101, 129, and 142.

[39] The Pilgrim Psalms (also known as the Song of Ascents or Gradual Psalms) are Psalms 120-134 (119-133 in the Septuagint and the Vulgate). Under the Rule of St. Benedict, these psalms were assigned to Terce, Sext and None on weekdays. One theory is that these psalms were recited by Jewish pilgrims on their way to Jerusalem to attend the three pilgrim festivals. Another theory is that they were sung by the Levites as they ascended the fifteen steps leading up to the Courtyard of the Priests in the Second Temple in Jerusalem; see https://en.wikipedia.org/wiki/Song_of_Ascents.

[40] "The Office of the Dead (*Officium defunctorum*) is another essential component of Books of Hours. The text is not that of the Requiem Mass (which belongs to the Missal) but of the prayers said over the coffin as it lies on a bier in the church choir during the wake-night or vigils before burial...The solemn celebration of death in late medieval times, so different from modern attitudes which trivialize the subject, was in part a reaction to the traumatic experience and memory of the Black Death and recurrent plagues; it was important to know how to die well.", John Harthan, The Book of Hours (Thomas Y. Crowell Company 1977), pg. 17.

[41] "… die Wagen … machten keinen Umweg um mich und rannten voll Verachtung über mich hin wie über eine schlechte Stelle, in der altes Wasser sich gesammelt hat. Und oft vor dem Einschlafen las ich das 30. Kapitel im Buch Hiob, und es war alles wahr an mir, Wort für Wort…" – Ruth Sieber-Rilke and Carl Sieber (ed.), Rainer Maria Rilke: Briefe aus den Jahren 1892-1904 (Insel-Verlag Leipzig 1939), pp. 360.

[42] "…indem nämlich aus jeder in Gebrauch genommenen Bedeutung Gott und Tod abgezogen schienen (als ein nicht Hiesiges, sondern Späteres, Anderwärtiges und Anderes), beschleunigte sich der kleinere Kreislauf des nur Hiesigen immer mehr, der sogenannte Fortschritt wurde zum Ereignis einer in sich befangenen Welt, die

Book of Hours created by the workshop
of Willem Vrelant (Ghent-Bruges, Belgium ca. 1460-1470)
Non-original "treasure binding" of boards covered with leather,
gilded metal (including medallions
showing the symbols of the four Evangelists),
and an ivory Christ (Frankfurt, Germany, 19th century)

vergass, dass sie, wie sie sich auch anstellte, durch den Tod und durch Gott von vornherein und endgültig übertroffen war. Nun hätte das noch eine Art Besinnung ergeben, wäre man imstande gewesen, Gott und Tod als blosse Ideen sich im Geistigen fernzuhalten –: aber die Natur wusste nichts von dieser uns irgendwie gelungenen Verdrängung – blüht ein Baum, so blüht so gut der Tod in ihm wie das Leben, und der Acker ist voller Tod, der aus seinem liegenden Gesicht einen reichen Ausdruck des Lebens treibt, und die Tiere gehen geduldig von einem [zum] anderen – und überall um uns ist der Tod noch zu Haus und aus den Ritzen der Dinge sieht er uns zu, und ein rostiger Nagel, der irgendwo aus einer Planke steht, tut Tag und Nacht nichts, als sich freuen über ihn." – Ruth Sieber-Rilke (ed.), <u>Rainer Maria Rilke: Briefe aus den Jahren 1914 - 1926</u> (Insel-Verlag 1950), pp. 55-56.

[43] "... [the] first half [of the prayer in the Suffrages] recounts an episode from the saint's life or touches on some important aspect of the saint's holiness; the second half of the prayer is always a petition for aid from God through the saint's intercession." - http://www.medievalbooksofhours.com/learn (under description of Suffrages).

[44] Ruth Sieber-Rilke and Carl Sieber (ed.), <u>Rainer Maria Rilke: Briefe aus den Jahren 1921 - 1926</u> (Insel-Verlag Leipzig 1935), pp. 130-131.

[45] For selections of poems in the original German from *Book of Monastic Life* allocated to the monastic hours of prayer and accompanied by modern black and white photographs and a music DVD, see Gotthard Fermor (ed.), <u>Rainer Maria Rilke Das Stunden-Buch</u> (Gütersloher Verlagshaus 2014); see also Gotthard Fermor (ed.), <u>Rainer Maria Rilke Das Buch von der Pilgerschaft</u> (Gütersloher Verlagshaus 2016), where Rilke's poems are not allocated to any monastic hours of prayer, but are accompanied by modern black and white photographs and a music DVD.

[46] See http://www.medievalbooksofhours.com/learn#advanced (under description of "Office of the Dead").

[47] "In Moskau merkte ich es zuerst: Dieses ist ein Land des unvollendeten Gottes, und aus allen Gebärden des Volkes strömt die Wärme seines Werdens wie ein unendlicher Segen aus." – RMR letter to Emil Faktor, 3 June, 1899; quoted in Günther Schiwy, <u>Rilke und die Religion</u> (Insel-Verlag 2006), pg. 83.

[48] "'Vollenden' ist auch im *Stunden-Buch* das Stichwort, das Rilkes künftiges Schaffen prägen wird. Indem der Mensch, vor allem der Künstler, durch sein Werk Vollendetes schafft, vollendet er dadurch sich selbst und Gott." ("'Completing' is also the keyword in the *Book of Hours* that characterizes Rilke's future work. By creating fulfillment through his work, man, above all the artist, thereby completes himself and God") – Gunther Schiwy, <u>Rilke und die Religion</u> (Insel-Verlag 2006), pg. 93.

[49] "Es gibt vielleicht nichts so Eifersüchtiges wie meinen Beruf; und nicht ein Mönchsleben wäre meines in eines Klosters Zusammenschluss und Abtrennung, wohl aber muss ich sehen, nach und nach zu einem Kloster auszuwachsen und so dazustehn in der Welt, mit Mauern um mich, aber mit Gott und den Heiligen in mir, mit sehr schönen Bildern under Geräten in mir, mit Höfen, um die ein Tanz von Säulen geht, mit Fruchtgärten, Weinbergen und Brunnen, deren Grund gar nicht zu finden ist." – Ruth Sieber-Rilke and Carl Sieber (ed.), <u>Rainer Maria Rilke: Briefe aus den Jahren 1904 - 1907</u> (Insel-Verlag 1939), pg. 208.

[50] Ralph Freedman, "Das Stunden-Buch and Das Buch der Bilder: Harbingers of Rilke's Maturity", in Erika Metzger and Michael Metzger (editors), <u>A Companion to the Works of Rainer Maria Rilke</u> (Camden House 2001), pg. 92.

[51] "Letzter Zuruf...Schweifst Du frei in's Ungewisse, so verantwortest nur Du für Dich selbst; indessen für den Fall, dass Du Dich bindest, musst Du erfahren, warum ich Dich auf einen so ganz bestimmten Weg zur

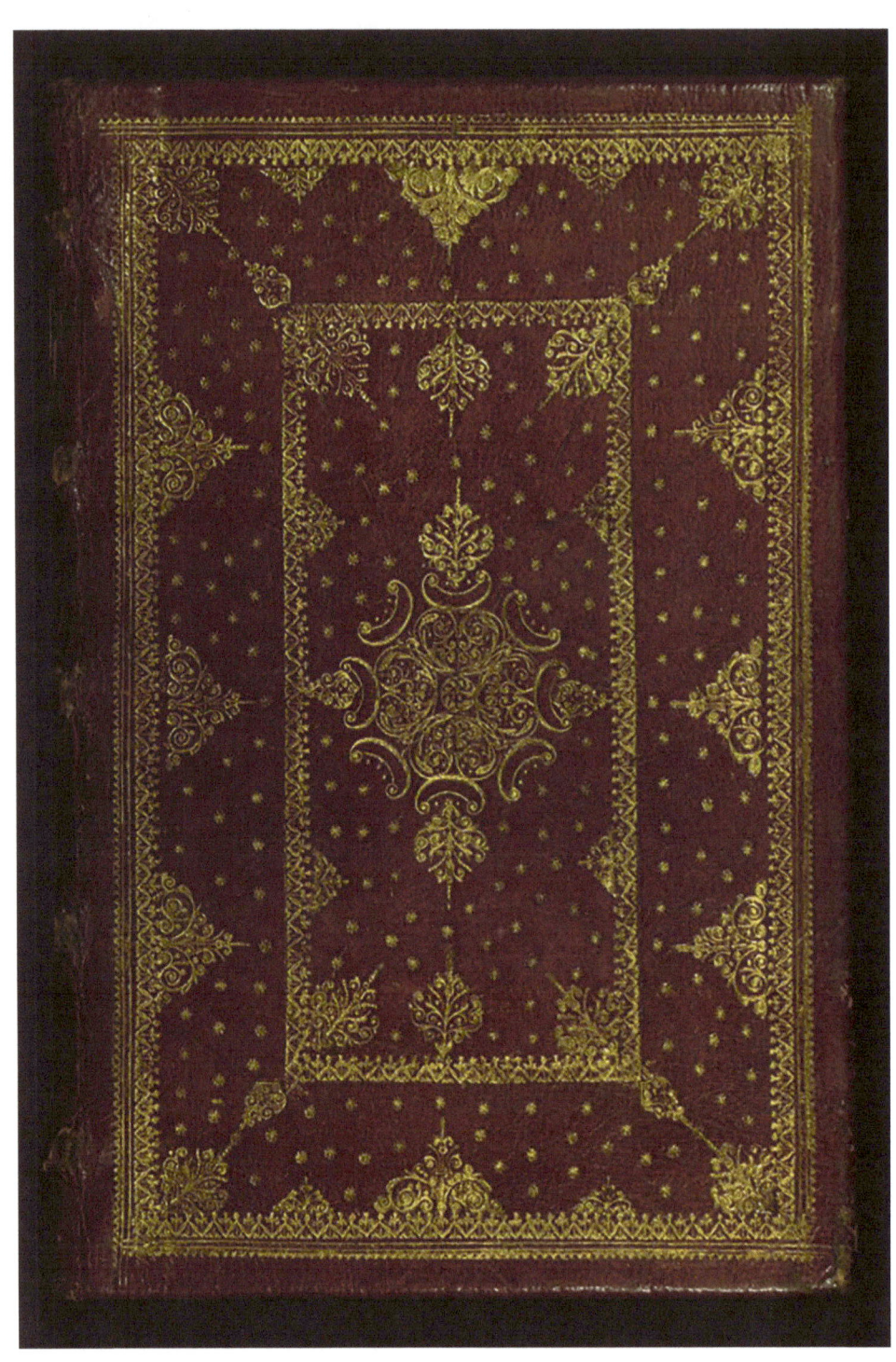

Book of Hours created by the Masters of the Gold Scrolls
for a patron devoted to Saint Francis
(Bruges, Belgium ca. 1440-1450)
Ink and pigments on parchment bound
between boards covered by leather

Gesundheit unermüdlich hinwies...In den 'Mönschsliedern', in manchen Zeiten früher, vorigen Winter, diesen Winter, standest Du heil vor mir! Begreifst Du meine Angst und meine Heftigkeit, wenn Du wieder abglittest ...Darum verlor Deine Gestalt, - in Wolfrathshausen noch so lieb und deutlich dicht vor mir, - sich mir mehr und mehr wie ein Einzeltheilchen in einer Gesammtlandschaft, - in einer weiten Wolgalandscaft gleichsam, und die kleine Hütte darin war nicht die Deine. Ich gehorchte ohne es zu wissen dem grossen Plan des Lebens...Mit tiefer Demuth nehme ich es entgegen: und weiss nun seherklar und rufe Dir zu: gehe denselben Weg Deinem dunklen Gott entgegen! Er kann, was ich nicht mehr thun kann an Dir, - und so lange schon nicht mehr mit voller Drangabe thun konnte: er kann Dich zur Sonne und Reife segnen." - Ernst Pfeiffer (ed.), Rainer Maria Rilke Lou Andreas-Salomé Briefwechsel (Insel-Verlag 1975), pp. 53-54.

[52] "...Lou and Rilke were not medieval lovers and they were not completely constrained by the sexual mores of their time. When they met, Lou had been married for ten years to a translator of Persian and specialist in Oriental languages, Friedrich Carl Andreas, who was fifteen years her senior. It was a marriage of peculiar convenience that Lou had finally consented to in order to save Andreas from his self-destructive urges. (In Lou's presence, he had once threatened to kill himself, plunging a knife into his chest.)" - Angela von der Lippe (translator), Lou Andreas-Salomé, You Alone are Real to Me: Remembering Rainer Maria Rilke (BOA Editions, Ltd. 2003), pg. 8.

[53] See Edward Snow and Michael Winkler, Rilke and Andreas-Salomé: A Love Story in Letters (W.W. Norton & Company 1975), page 7: "May 31/June 1: RMR and LAS make a two-day excursion to the village of Wolfratshausen, south of Munich near Lake Starnberg, in search of a retreat near the mountains for a longer sojourn. During this trip they almost certainly become lovers."

[54] See Stéphane Michaud and Dorothee Pfeiffer (ed.), Lou Andreas-Salomé, Russland mit Rainer: Tagebuch der Reise mit Rainer Maria Rilke im Jahre 1900 (Deutsche Schillergesellschaft 1999), for Salomé's diary of their 1900 trip to Russia.

[55] See https://en.wikipedia.org/wiki/Dormition_Cathedral,_Moscow.

[56] See https://en.wikipedia.org/wiki/Kiev_Pechersk_Lavra; see also, the description of Rilke's visit contained in Annemarie Kidder, The Book of Hours: Prayers to a Lowly God (Northwestern University Press 2001), pp. xvii – xviii.

[57] "Erforschen Sie den Grund, der Sie schreiben heisst; prüfen Sie, ob er in der tiefsten Stelle Ihres Herzens seine Wurzeln asusstreckt, gestehen Sie sich ein, ob Sie sterben müssten, wenn es Ihnen versagt würde zu schreiben. Dieses vor allem: fragen Sie sich in der stillsten Stunde Ihrer Nacht: muss ich schreiben? Graben Sie in sich nach einer tiefen Antwort. Und wenn diese zustimmend lauten sollte, wenn Sie mit einem starken und einfachen 'Ich muss' dieser ernsten Frage begegnen dürfen, dann bauen Sie Ihr Leben nach dieser Notwendigkeit..." Ruth Sieber-Rilke (ed.), Rainer Maria Rilke: Briefe 1897 - 1914 (Insel-Verlag 1950), pp. 41-42.

[58] Ernst Pfeiffer (editor), Rainer Maria Rilke Lou Andreas Salomé Briefwechsel (Insel-Verlag 1975); for a translation into English, see Edward Snow and Michael Winkler, Rilke and Andreas-Salomé: A Love Story in Letters (W.W. Norton and Company 1975).

[59] "Over the entire span of the poems' composition he kept them a secret from everyone – except Lou, to whom he went to great lengths to entrust them (there are times when she may have had the *only* copies), and to whom he always referred to them as 'Prayers' (*Gebete*). It was only in 1905, when Rilke decided on publication, that he retrieved the sequences from Lou and shaped them into their present form." - Edward Snow, The Poetry of Rilke (North Point Press 2009), Translator's Commentary, pp. 624-627.

Book of Hours created in northeastern France,
possibly for the marriage
of Louis I of Châtillon (d. 1346) and Jeanne of Hainaut
ink and pigments on parchment bound
between boards covered by leather

[60] "Einst sagte man schlankweg: 'alle Religion entsteht aus der Wechselbeziehung zwischen Gott und Menschen'...Indem man vom Menschen ausgeht, anstatt wie einst vom Gott, übersieht man fast unwillkührlich, dass das eigentliche religiöse Phänomen in der That erst gegeben ist in der Rückwirkung einer, gleichviel wie entstandenen, Gottheit auf den an sie glaubenden Menschen...Nun kann es sich aber ereignen, dass das, was ein religiöses Genie ganz heimlich nnd individuell in seinem Innern erlebt, durch ein besonders glückliches Zusammentreffen von Zeiten, Umständen und historischen Zufälligkeiten, ausnahmsweise einmal in seinen Gottes vorstellungen völlig nach aussen gelangt, — sich den absolut adäquaten Ausdruck in Worten und Bildern schafft, so dass also, wie etwas in dem Werk eines Dichters dessen höchster künstlerischer Traum, der höchste religiöse Traum der Menschheit uns in seiner ganzen Vollendung gleichsam greifbar, plastisch geworden, entgegentritt." – Lou Andreas-Salomé, "Jesu der Jude", Neue Deutsche Rundschau, Volume 7, Part I (1896), pp. 342-344.

[61] "Mir war wie einem, dem grosse Träume in Erfüllung gehen mit ihrem Guten und Bösen; denn Ihr *Essay* verhielt sich zu meinen Gedichten wie Traum zu Wirklichkeit wie ein Wunsch zur Erfüllung." - Ernst Pfeiffer (editor), Rainer Maria Rilke Lou Andreas Salomé Briefwechsel (Insel-Verlag 1975), pg. 7.

[62] "From wills and inventories it is clear that Books of Hours were regarded as important, precious objects...For the living, the most obvious occasion for acquiring a Book of Hours was on marriage. Prayerbooks were frequently commissioned or bought as a wedding present from a husband to his bride...These 'wedding' Books of Hours started a fashion which survived for centuries. On the occasion of the marriage of her second son Alfred, Duke of Edinburgh, to the Czar's daughter in 1874, Queen Victoria sent a plain and an illuminated prayerbook to St. Petersburg, the first for the groom, the second for the bride." John Harthan, The Book of Hours (Thomas Y. Crowell Company 1977), pg. 34; and "Because Books of Hours were such personal items, in daily use and often a gift or bequest from loved ones, they were an especially appropriate place for gestures of affection."- Eamon Duffy, Marking the Hours: English People & Their Prayers 1240-1570 (Yale University Press 2006), pg. 49.

[63] "War ich jahrelang Deine Frau, so deshalb, weil Du mir *das erstmalig Wirkliche* gewesen bist, Leib und Mensch ununterscheidbar eins, unbezweifelbarer Tatbestand des Lebens selbst. Wortwörtlich hätte ich Dir bekennen können, was Du gesagt hast als Dein Liebesbekenntnis: 'Du allein bist wirklich'. Darin wurden wir Gatten, noch ehe wir Freunde geworden, und befreundet wurden wir kaum aus Wahl, sondern aus ebenso untergründig vollzogenen Vermählungen. Nicht zwei Hälften suchten sich in uns: die überraschte Ganzheit erkannte sich erschauernd an unfasslicher Ganzheit." - Lou Andreas-Salomé, Lebensrückblick ("Looking Back at Life") (Insel-Verlag 1968), pg. 138 (Nachtrag "Epilogue", 1934).

[64] Lou Andreas-Salomé, Lebensrückblick ("Looking Back at Life"), pp. 139-140 (Nachtrag "Epilogue", 1934).

[65] See https://en.wikipedia.org/wiki/Song_of_Songs.

[66] See Karl Webb, "Rainer Maria Rilke and the Visual Arts", in Erika Metzger and Michael Metzger (editors), A Companion to the Works of Rainer Maria Rilke (Camden House 2001), pp 264-288.

[67] Ruth Sieber-Rilke und Carl Sieber, Rainer Maria Rilke, Tagebücher aus der Frühzeit (Insel-Verlag 1942), pp. 13-140; for an English translation, see Edward Snow and Michael Winkler, Rainer Maria Rilke: Diaries of a Young Poet (W.W. Norton and Company 1997), pp. 1-78.

[68] "Russiche Kunst" ("Russian Art"), in Die Zeit (Wochenschrift) XXIX. Band 368, Vienna, 19 October 1901; see http://gutenberg.spiegel.de/buch/von-kunst-dingen-818/11.

[69] See https://www.russianartandculture.com/rilke-und-russland.

Book of Hours in the style of the Master of the Prayerbook
(Bruges, Belgium ca. 1500)
prayer inscribed by first owner "Philip"
confessing to be a sinner and asking for his heart to be pure
ink and pigments on parchment bound between
boards covered with velvet

[70] Rainer Maria Rilke, Worpswede: Monographie einer Landschaft und ihrer Maler, at http://gutenberg.spiegel.de/buch/worpswede-830/1.

[71] "Ich sehe bei Rodin, was das für ihn bedeutet, dass alles Seine so immer um ihn ist...Das ist eines seiner Geheimnisse, oder vielmehr einer der Stützen seiner Grösse...Aber vor allem die Arbeit. Was man bei Rodin fühlt: sie ist Raum, sie ist Zeit, sie ist Wand, sie ist Traum, sie ist Fenster und Ewigkeit...*Il faut travailler toujours*...Neulich, Sonnabend, sagte er das, und wie er das sagte, so tief überzeugt, so schlicht, so aus der Arbeit heraus, - es war nur wie ein Geräusch und ein Rühren seiner Hände." - Ruth Sieber-Rilke and Carl Sieber (ed.), Rainer Maria Rilke: Briefe aus den Jahren 1902-1906 (Insel-Verlag 1929), pp. 42-43.

[72] Rachel Corbett, You Must Change Your Life: The Story of Rainer Maria Rilke and Auguste Rodin (W. W. Norton & Company 2016), pg 85.

[73] For an English translation of the collected letters, see Joel Agee (translator), Rainer Maria Rilke: Letters on Cézanne (North Point Press 2002).

[74] Ruth Sieber-Rilke und Carl Sieber, Rainer Maria Rilke, Tagebücher aus der Frühzeit (Insel-Verlag 1942); Ruth Sieber-Rilke und Carl Sieber, Rainer Maria Rilke, Briefe und Tagebücher aus der Frühzeit 1899-1902 (Insel-Verlag 1931); for an English translation, see Edward Snow and Michael Winkler, Rainer Maria Rilke: Diaries of a Young Poet (W.W. Norton and Company 1997).

[75] Ernst Pfeiffer (editor), Rainer Maria Rilke Lou Andreas-Salomé Briefwechsel (Insel-Verlag 1975); Ruth Sieber-Rilke and Carl Sieber (ed.), Rainer Maria Rilke: Briefe aus den Jahren 1892 - 1904 (Insel-Verlag 1939); Ruth Sieber-Rilke and Carl Sieber (ed.), Rainer Maria Rilke: Briefe aus den Jahren 1899 - 1902 (Insel-Verlag 1931); Ruth Sieber-Rilke and Carl Sieber (ed.), Rainer Maria Rilke: Briefe aus den Jahren 1902-1906 (Insel-Verlag 1930); Ruth Sieber-Rilke and Carl Sieber (ed.), Rainer Maria Rilke: Briefe aus den Jahren 1904 - 1907 (Insel-Verlag 1939); Ruth Sieber-Rilke and Carl Sieber (ed.), Rainer Maria Rilke: Briefe aus den Jahren 1906 - 1907 (Insel-Verlag 1930); Ruth Sieber-Rilke and Carl Sieber (ed.), Rainer Maria Rilke: Briefe aus den Jahren 1907-1914 (Insel-Verlag 1933); Ruth Sieber-Rilke and Carl Sieber (ed.), Rainer Maria Rilke: Briefe aus Muzot 1921-1926 (Insel-Verlag 1935); Ruth Sieber-Rilke (ed.), Rainer Maria Rilke Briefe (Erster Band: 1897-1914; Zweiter Band: 1914-1926)(Insel-Verlag 1950); Ruth Sieber-Rilke und Carl Sieber (ed.), Rainer Maria Rilke: Briefe an seinen Verleger (in zwei Bänden: 1906-1926) (Insel-Verlag 1949); for English translations of some letters, see Jane Greene and M.D. Herter Norton, Letters of Rainer Maria Rilke (Volume One: 1892-1910; Volume Two: 1910-1926) (W.W. Norton & Company 1948); Edward Snow and Michael Winkler, Rilke and Andreas-Salomé: A Love Story in Letters (W.W. Norton and Company 1975); Stephen Mitchell, Rainer Maria Rilke: Letters to a Young Poet (The Modern Library 1984).

[76] "Wenn ich hinaufkäme zu Euch, so würde ich gewiss auch den Prunk von Moor und Heide, das schwebend helle Grün der Wiesenstücke und die Birken neu und anders sehen; zwar hat diese Verwandlung, da ich sie einmal ganz erlebte und teilte, einen Teil des Stunden-Buchs hervorgerufen; aber damals war mir die Natur noch ein allgemeiner Anlass, eine Evokation, ein Instrument, in dessen Saiten sich meine Hände wiederfanden; ich sass noch nicht vor ihr; ich liess mich hinreissen von der Seele, welche von ihr ausging; sie kam über mich mit ihrer Weite, mit ihrem grossen übertriebenen Dasein, wie das Prophezeien über Saul kam; genau so. Ich schritt einher und sah, sah nicht die Natur, sondern die Gesichte, die sie mir eingab." - Ruth Sieber-Rilke (ed.), Rainer Maria Rilke: Briefe aus den Jahren 1897 - 1914 (Insel-Verlag 1950), pp. 198-199.

[77] "Nach dem Gehaste der Stadt wieder diesen hohen wartenden Wald zu sehen! Wie vornehm ist doch das Stehen, die Ruhe, Verwirrt von den heftigen Gesten der Menschen, fühlt man, dass es nur zwei verwandte und grosse Bewegungen gibt. Der Flügelschlag eines hohen Vogels und das Schwanken der Wipfel. Diese beiden

Book of Hours (Use of Rome) created by an artist
in the circle of Wllem Vrelant (Bruges, Belgium ca. 1460-1470)
ink and pigments on parchment bound
between boards covered in leather

Gebärden sollen deine Seele lehren, sich zu bewegen." - Ruth Sieber-Rilke und Carl Sieber, <u>Rainer Maria Rilke, Tagebücher aus der Frühzeit</u> (Insel-Verlag 1942), pp. 218-219.

[78] "Ich fing mich mit den Dingen an, die die eigentlichen Vertrauten meiner einsamen Kindheit gewesen sind, und es war schon viel, dass ich es, ohne fremde Hilfe, bis zu den Tieren gebracht habe…Dann aber tat sich mir Russland auf und schenkte mir die Brüderlichkeit und das Dunkel Gottes, in dem allein Gemeinschaft ist. So nannte ich ihn damals auch, den über mich hereingebrochenen Gott, und lebte lange im Vorraum seines Namens, auf den Knieen…Jetzt würdest Du mich ihn kaum ne nennen hören, es ist eine unbeschreibliche Diskretion zwischen uns, und wo einmal Nähe war und Durchdringung, da spannen sich neue Fernen, so wie im Atom, das die neue Wissenschaft auch als ein Weltall im Kleinen begreift. Das Fassliche entgeht, verwandelt sich, statt des Besitzes erlernt man den Bezug, und es entsteht eine Namenlosigkeit, die wieder bei Gott beginnen muss, um vollkommen und ohne Ausrede zu sein. Das Gefühlserlebnis tritt zurück hinter einer unendlichen Lust zu allem Fühlbaren…, die Eigenschaften werden Gott, dem nicht mehr Sagbaren, abgenommen, fallen zurück an die Schöpfung, an Liebe und Tod…es ist vielleicht immer wieder nur das, was schon an gewissen Stellen im Stundenbuch sich vollzog, dieser Aufstieg Gottes aus dem atmenden Herzen, davon sich der Himmel bedeckt, und sein Niederfall als Regen." –Ruth Sieber-Rilke (ed.), <u>Rainer Maria Rilke: Briefe aus den Jahren 1914-1926</u> (Insel-Verlag 1950), pg 395.

[79] "Wenn Gott ein Gesetz gegeben hat, so lautet es: Sei einsam von Zeit zu Zeit. Denn er kann nur zu einem kommen oder zu zweien, die er nicht mehr unterscheiden kann." - Ruth Sieber-Rilke und Carl Sieber, <u>Rainer Maria Rilke: Tagebücher aus der Frühzeit</u> (Insel-Verlag 1942), pg. 203.

[80] <u>The Holy Bible, Revised Standard Version (Second Catholic Edition)</u> (Ignatius Press 2006).

[81] See http://www.ordinariate.org.uk/news/OrdinariateNews.php?Mgr-Andrew-Burnham-The-Customary-of-Our-Lady-of-Walsingham-121.

[82] See https://ordinariate.net.

[83] See http://prelaturaspersonales.org/wp-content/uploads/2012/02/Calendar_for_Ordinariate.pdf.

[84] Selten ist Sonne im Sobór.
Die Wände wachsen aus Gestalten,
und durch die Jungfraun und die Alten
drängt sich, wie Flügel im Entfalten,
das goldene, das Kaiser-Tor.

An seinem Säulenrand verlor
die Wand sich hinter den Ikonen;
und, die im stillen Silber wohnen,
die Steine, steigen wie ein Chor
und fallen wieder in die Kronen
und schweigen schöner als zuvor.

Und über sie, wie Nächte blau,
von Angesichte blass,
schwebt, die dich freuete, die Frau:
die Pförtnerin, der Morgentau,

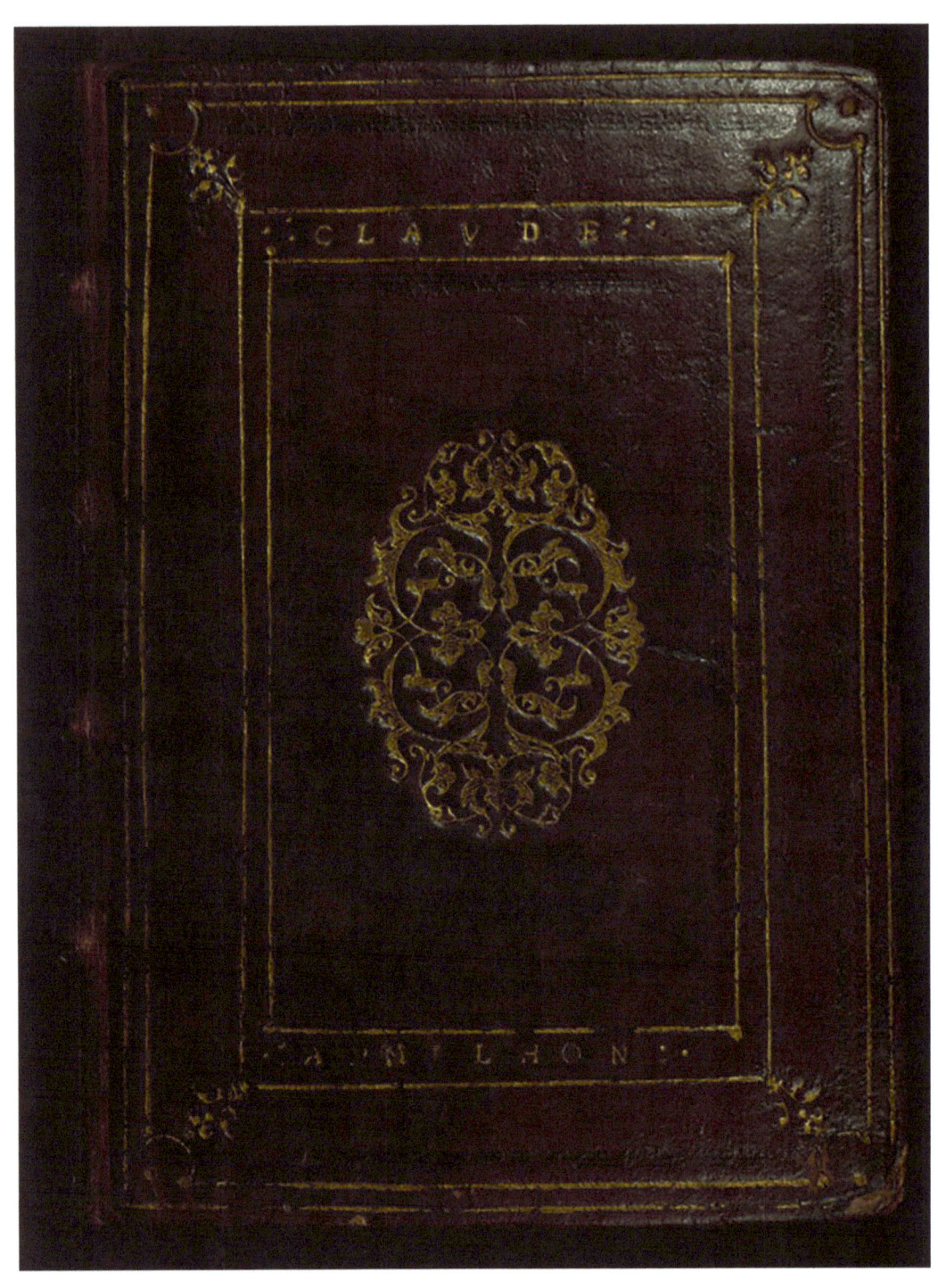

Book of Hours (Use of Reims) (Northeastern France ca. 1450-1475)
First owner Colette is portrayed on Folio 76r with Virgin and Child
Ink and pigments on parchment bound
between boards covered with leather

die dich umblüht wie eine Au
und ohne Unterlass.

Die Kuppel ist voll deines Sohns
und bindet rund den Bau.

Willst du geruhen deines Throns,
den ich in Schauern schau.

⁸⁵ Uspensky Sobor:

⁸⁶ For an extensive discussion of Rilke's use of rhythm and metre and other features of his poetry, see Susan Ranson (translator) and Ben Hutchinson (Editor), <u>Rainer Maria Rilke's The Book of Hours: A New Translation with Commentary</u> (Camden House 2008), pp. xxxv - xliii.

⁸⁷ Walter Benjamin, "The Task of the Translator", <u>Illuminations</u> (Pimlico 1999), pg. 79.

⁸⁸ "Der Himmel war von weichem Grau mit wenigen hellen Spalten und Sprüngen, von denen überhellt das Land nach allen Seiten hin tief und weit war. Wie biblische Landschaften waren die Fernen mit Bergen, Baumgruppen und Wasserläufen…Einfach in der Kontur, nicht irgendeine Gegend, einfach: die Erde. Die Erde, in welche die Völker sind zerstreut worden wie Staub im Sturm. Die Erde, die dem Menschen zu gross ist, die unter seinem Wandern in die Himmel wächst und über Tage und Nächte hinaus und die jenseits der Meere immer wieder beginnt und wächst, diese biblische fremde Erde, die Erde, die Gott noch in der Hand hält und die deshalb ohne Anfang und Absehen ist. Sehr dunkel und stumpf stand die Heide da, sanft wie japanische Seide das schüttere Gras, metallisch rot das gemähte Buchweizenfeld, dunkel und schwer das umgeackerte Land." - Ruth Sieber-Rilke und Carl Sieber, <u>Rainer Maria Rilke: Tagebücher aus der Frühzeit</u> (Insel-Verlag 1942), pg. 337.

Book of Hours (Use of Reims) (Northern France 15th century)
Scribe identified as Paulinus de Sorcy
Early 19th century binding by J. Bold & Sons, Bristol, England
Dark brown leather over pasteboards, geometric gilt pattern

[89] "... an jenem Abend, als wir zusammen im kleinen blauen Esszimmerchen sassen, sprachen wir auch von anderen Dingen: im kleinem Häuschen würde Licht sein, eine sanfte verhüllte Lampe, und ich würde an meinem Kocher stehen und Ihnen ein Abendbrot bereiten...Rote Mandarinen müssten da sein, in welche ein Sommer ganz klein zusammengefaltet ist, wie ein italienisches Seidentuch in eine Nussschale. Und Rosen wären um uns, hohe, welches sich von Zweigen neigen, und liegende, die leise ihre Häupter heben, und solche, die wandern von Hand zu Hand, wie Mädchen in einem Tanzspiel. So träumte ich. Voreilige Träume, das Häuschen ist leer und kalt, und auch meine hiesige Wohnung ist leer und kalt: Gott Weiss, wie sie wohnlich warden soll. – Aber dennoch kann ich nicht glauben, dass die Wirklichkeit gar nicht soll Beziehung gewinnen zu dem, was ich träumte." – Ruth Sieber-Rilke und Carl Sieber, Rainer Maria Rilke: Briefe und Tagebücher aus der Frühzeit 1899 - 1902 (Insel-Verlag 1931), pp. 56-57.

[90] "Alles ist, wie ich schon schrieb, zu einer Angelegenheit der Farben untereinander geworden: eine nimmt sich gegen die andere zusammen, betont sich ihr gegenüber, besinnt sich auf sich selbst...schwächere Lokalfarben geben sich ganz auf und begnügen sich damit, die stärkste vorhandene zu spiegeln. In diesem Hin und Wider von gegenseitigem vielartigem Einfluss schwingt das Bild-innere, steigt und fällt in sich selbst zurück und hat nicht eine stehende Stelle." Ruth Sieber-Rilke (ed.), Rainer Maria Rilke: Briefe 1897 - 1914 (Insel-Verlag 1950), pg. 218.

[91] "Auf der anderen Seite in der blauen Decke aus einer vom Blau bestimmten Porzellanschale teilweise herausgerollte Äpfel. Dass ihr Rot in das Blau hineinrollt, erscheint als eine Aktion, die so sehr aus den farbigen Vorgängen des Bildes zu stammen scheint, wie die Verbindung zweier Rodinscher Akte aus ihrer plastischen Affinität. Und zum Schluss noch eine Landschaft aus Luftblau, blauem Meer, roten Dächern, auf Grün miteinander sprechend und sehr bewegt in der inneren Unterhaltung, voller Mitteilung gegeneinander." Ruth Sieber-Rilke (ed.), Rainer Maria Rilke: Briefe 1897 - 1914 (Insel-Verlag 1950), pg. 225.

[92] "The couple was not well off; the old 'study grant' left René a decade before by his uncle Jaroslav had been withdrawn by his Prague cousins, and what little his father could send him was about to dry up...." – George Schoolfield, Young Rilke and His Time (Camden House 2009), pg. 134.

[93] See Rule of Saint Benedict, translated by Rev. Boniface Verheyen, OSB (1949 edition) at https://www.ecatholic2000.com/benedict/rule.shtml.

[94] "...[I]ch möchte Sie... bitten...zu versuchen, die Fragen selbst liebzuhaben wie verschlossene Stuben und wie Bücher, die in einer sehr fremden Sprache geschrieben sind. Forschen Sie jetzt nicht nach den Antworten, die Ihnen nicht gegeben werden können, weil Sie nicht leben könnten. Und es handelt sich darum, alles zu leben. Leben Sie jetzt die Fragen. Vielleicht leben Sie dann allmählich, ohne es zu merken, eines fernen Tages in die Antwort hinein." - Ruth Sieber-Rilke (ed.), Rainer Maria Rilke: Briefe aus den Jahren 1897 - 1914 (Insel-Verlag 1950), pg. 49.

[95] "Wer den Glauben nicht hat, hat die Kraft nicht." - Ruth Sieber-Rilke und Carl Sieber, Rainer Maria Rilke: Tagebücher aus der Frühzeit (Insel-Verlag 1942), pg. 43.

[96] "Diese letzte Woche bin ich jeden Tag von 10 Uhr an bis 5 Uhr nachmittags in der Nationalbibliothek gewesen und habe viele Bücher gelesen und viele Reproduktionen von Kathedralen aus dem XII. und XIII. Jahrhundert gesehen. Du, das war eine grosse, grosse Kunst. Je mehr man sich mit ihren Dingen befasst, desto tiefer fühlt man den Wert und die Köstlichkeit der Arbeit: denn diese Kathedralen, diese Berge und Gebirge des Mittelalters, wären nie fertig geworden, wenn sie aus Inspirationen hätten entstehen sollen. Da musste ein Tag wie der andere kommen und Hand anlegen, und wenn nicht jeder eine Inspiration war, so war doch jeder ein Weg dazu." - Ruth Sieber-Rilke and Carl Sieber (ed.), Rainer Maria Rilke: Briefe aus den Jahren 1892 - 1904 (Insel-Verlag 1939), pp. 269-270.

Book of Hours in Dutch (Haarlem, Netherlands 15th century) brown, oiled leather with a roll border with silver design, cast and chiselled metal corner pieces and clasps

[97] "Am weitesten von allem sind die Sternennächte, die mondlos im Dunkel aufblühn und gleitende Sterne hinstreuen aus Überfluss: solche, die rasch und plötzlich abfallen und, als fielen sie in Wasser, unversehens ausgehen; brennende, die aus einem Stern springen und, als hätten sie ihren Sprung abgemessen, in einen anderen Stern hinein, und stille, die gleich Vögeln mit ausgehaltenen Flügeln in flachem Bogen quer durch die Himmel schweben, zwischen zwei Sternen auftauchend, zwei anderen verschwindend, als wären diese Himmel nur ein Durchgang für sie, in dem sie sich nicht aufhalten." – Ruth Sieber-Rilke and Carl Sieber (ed.), Rainer Maria Rilke: Briefe aus den Jahren 1906 - 1907 (Insel-Verlag 1930), pg. 240.

[98] "Wir haben keinen Grund, gegen unsere Welt Misstrauen zu haben, denn sie ist nicht gegen uns. Hat sie Schrecken, so sind es unsere Schrecken, hat sie Abgründe, so gehören diese Abgründe uns, sind Gefahren da, so müssen wir versuchen, sie zu lieben. Und wenn wir nur unser Leben nach jenem Grundsatze einrichten, der uns rät, dass wir uns immer an das Schwere halten müssen, so wird das, welches uns jetzt noch als das Fremdeste erscheint, unser Vertrautestes und Treuestes werden. Wie sollten wir jener alten Mythen vergessen können, die am Anfange aller Völker stehen, der Mythen von den Drachen, die sich im äussersten Augenblick in Prinzessinnen verwandeln; vielleicht sind all Drachen unseres Lebens Prinzessinnen, die nur darauf warten, uns einmal schön und mutig zu sehen." – Ruth Sieber-Rilke (ed.), Rainer Maria Rilke: Briefe aus den Jahren 1897 - 1914 (Insel-Verlag 1950), pp. 101-102.

[99] "... sie öffnet sich und es entsteht jener *Johannes* mit den redenden, erregten Armen, mit dem grossen Gehen dessen, der einen Anderen hinter sich kommen fühlt. Der Körper dieses Mannes ist nichtmehr unerprobt: die Wüsten haben ihn durchglüht, der Hunger hat ihm weh getan, und alle Dürste haben ihn geprüft. Er hat bestanden und ist hart geworden. Sein hagerer Asketenleib ist wie ein Holzgriff, in dem die weite Gabel seines Schrittes steckt. Er geht. Er geht, als wären alle Weiten der Welt in ihm und als teilte er sie aus mit seinem Gehen. Er geht. Seine Arme sagen von diesem Gang und seine Finger spreizen sich und scheinen in der Luft das Zeichen des Schreitens zu machen." Ernst Zinn (editor), Rainer Maria Rilke Sämtliche Werke in Zwölf Bänden, Band 9 (Insel Verlag 1975), pg. 161.

[100] "...alle diese Stücke, jedes in seiner Art, enthalten Annäherungen an die Grenzempfindungen des Daseins und streben alle jenem ahnbaren Ausgleich zu, den ich am Unvergleichlichsten einmal in einem Fragment antiker Musik dargestellt gefunden habe. Romain Rolland, der es mir vorspielte, hatte es in einer gregorianischen Messe entdeckt. Da ich es vernahm und wiedervernahm, hatte ich den Eindruck zweier Waagschalen, die, leise ausschwebend, gegen einander zur Ruhe kamen. Ich schilderte Rolland meine Empfindung, und da erst gestand er mir, dass es sich um eine antike Grabschrift, eine Grabschrift in Noten handle: für die das dann allerdings die ergreifendste Bestätigung war, dass sie unter solchem Gleichnis konnte aufgenommen under verstanden werden." - Ruth Sieber-Rilke (ed.), Rainer Maria Rilke: Briefe aus den Jahren 1914-1926 (Insel-Verlag 1950), pg. 122.

[101] "Ein Baum aber ist doch im Garten, der auch im Toskanischen, in einem alten Kloster, stehen könnte: eine hohe alte Zypresse, ganz durchwachsen von einem Zug von Glyzinien, die nun überall, bis hoch hinauf, aus dem Dunkel des Baumes ihre leichten blauvioletten Gehänge steigen und fallen lassen - ; das ist Freude. Das und die herrlichen Feigenbäume, die wie Altarleuchter aus dem alten Testament mit den rundaufgebogenen Ästen dastehen und langsam ihre lichtgrünen Blätter aufschlagen." – Ruth Sieber-Rilke and Carl Sieber (ed.), Rainer Maria Rilke: Briefe aus den Jahren 1902-1906 (Insel-Verlag 1930), pg. 147.

[102] "Lassen Sie sich nicht beirren durch die Oberflächen; in den Tiefen wird alles Gesetz. Und die das Geheimnis falsch und schlecht leben (und es sind sehr viele), verlieren es nur für sich selbst und geben es doch weiter wie einen verschlossenen Brief, ohne es zu wissen." - Ruth Sieber-Rilke (ed.), Rainer Maria Rilke: Briefe aus den Jahren 1897 - 1914 (Insel-Verlag 1950), pg. 51.

Book of Hours for a member of the Catalonian Almogàver family
(Spain ca. 1510-1520)
Rebound ca. 1835 with reddish brown morocco; blind-tooled and stamped with gold; upper and lower boards include gilded bands of feathers along outer edges

[103] "…nun hatten wir wieder ein paar Tage grosser Sonne, und heute ist Regen, und gegenüber, über der Mauer, die Blätter der Kastanienbäume und der Akazien wendet ein leichter Wind, so dass sie von allen Seiten das Regnen haben und fühlen und glänzen davon. Und es ist einer von den Regentagen, die nicht für die Stadt sind. Die man draussen erleben müsste, all das verdunkelte Grün zu sehen, alle die Wiesen, die Grau spiegeln, alle die Buchenblätter, die bewegt sind und vielfältiger im Grün, seit die Lichter nicht mehr da sind (die hellen, schmelzenden, auflösenden Lichter), die nur Reflexe haben, Grün, das sich wieder in Grün schaut, Grün, das, auf Grün gestellt, grüne Schatten hat, Grün, das tief geworden ist und irgendwo einen Grund hat schliesslich, einen Grund von Grün. Und auf einmal ist auch aus dem Duft alles Farbige herausgenommen, als ob die Sonne im Fortgehen es fallen gelassen hätte in die Blumen hinein. Nun duften die Blätter, die kleinen Buchenblätter vor allem, und die altmodischen Blätter der Ulmen und die kleinen umgestürzten Blätter der Balsampappeln fliessen langsam aus in die Luft hinein." – Ruth Sieber-Rilke and Carl Sieber (ed.), Rainer Maria Rilke: Briefe aus den Jahren 1904 - 1907 (Insel-Verlag 1939), pp. 149-150.

[104] "Auf dem Wege nach Pietra Santa gibt es einem blutenden Berg. Wie ein verstaubtes Pilgerkleid schiebt er die Oliven zurück von dem steingrauen Leib und zeigt dem verträumten Tal, das nicht an ihn hat glauben wollen, die Wunde in der Brust: roter Marmor, in grauem Körper eingesprengt." - Ruth Sieber-Rilke und Carl Sieber, Rainer Maria Rilke: Tagebücher aus der Frühzeit (Insel-Verlag 1942), pg. 94.

[105] "Wenn Gott ein Gesetz gegeben hat, so lautet es: Sei einsam von Zeit zu Zeit. Denn er kann nur zu einem kommen oder zu zweien, die er nicht mehr unterscheiden kann." - Ruth Sieber-Rilke und Carl Sieber, Rainer Maria Rilke: Tagebücher aus der Frühzeit (Insel-Verlag 1942), pg. 203.

[106] "Jetzt ist es Herbst bei Dir, und Du gehst im Wald, im grossen Wald, in den man schon so weit hineinsehen kann, im Wind, der die Welt verwandelt…I denke an die Abende, nach denen die Sturmnacht kommt, die alles Welke aus den Bäumen nimmt, und denke an den Sturm selbst, an die Nacht, die fliegt, an den Sternen vorbei in den Morgen hinein. In den leeren, neuen, klaren, ausgestürmten Morgen…." – Ruth Sieber-Rilke and Carl Sieber (ed.), Rainer Maria Rilke: Briefe aus den Jahren 1892-1904 (Insel-Verlag 1939), pg. 406.

[107] "Und so viel Grund ich auch hätte, mich zum Schreibpult zu zwingen, so geh ich doch immer wieder mit, wenn der Morgen plötzlich irgendwo draussen ruft, so dass man meint, dort irgendwo müsste noch ein anderer sein, ein ganz grosser Morgen, der Morgen der Möwen und der Inselvögel, der Morgen der Abhänge und der unerreichbaren Blumen, jener immer gleiche ewige Morgen, der noch nicht mit Menschen rechnen muss, die ihn, aus ihrer Vorfrühstücksstimmung heraus, zweideutig und misstrauisch und kritisierend anblinzeln. Und man muss nur eine halbe Stunde gehen, mit jenen raschen, leichten, frühen Schritten, die einen so unbegreiflich weit bringen, um ihn wirklich um sich zu haben, den Meermorgen, der sicher ist, dass alles in ihm mit ihm ist und nichts gegen ihn; dass in seinem Aufgehen tausendmal and tausendmal seine eigene Gebärde sich wiederholt, bis sie in den kleinen Blumen sich verlangsamt under gleichsam zusammenfasst." - Ruth Sieber-Rilke (ed.), Rainer Maria Rilke: Briefe aus den Jahren 1897 - 1914 (Insel-Verlag 1950), pp. 165-166.

[108] "Worauf ich sagte, dass ich es als glücklichen Fortschritt anerkenne, dass hinter uns nicht mehr mit den Zeiten des Jahres frohe und traurige Hintergründe stehen, die mit teilnahmsloser Regelmässigkeit abwechseln. Dass wir traurige Frühlinge sehen und selige Herbsttage voll Überfluss und Freude, dass Sommertage schwer sein können und öde und grenzenlos und das der Winter uns berühren kann in unserem Gefühl, wie der Klang eines Triangel, wie Silber auf Damast, wie Rosen auf einem Mädchenhals…Das macht, dass wir ruhiger und in tieferen Verständnis mit der Natur, d.h. unbewusster hinleben können. Wenn hinter unserer Traurigkeit ein schimmernder Frühling flimmert und in hohen Wolken sich bewegt, dann wird unsere Traurigkeit rührender sein, und gross ist unser purpurnes Gefühl, wenn es sich aus fallenden Blättern Kränze formt und alle Farben des Oktobers verbraucht, abgelöst von ihrem Sinne im Absterben." - Ruth Sieber-Rilke und Carl Sieber, Rainer Maria Rilke: Tagebücher aus der Frühzeit (Insel-Verlag 1942), pg. 324.

Book of Hours in Dutch created by the
"Sarijs group" of the Brethren of the Common Life
(Zwolle, Netherlands, ca. 1470)
ink and pigments on parchment covered with late seventeenth-century
Dutch binding; cream-colored vellum over pasteboard, gold-tooled

[109] "So schlecht lebt man doch, weil man in die Gegenwart immer unfertig kommt, unfähig und zu allem zerstreut. Ich kann an keine Zeit meines Lebens zurückdenken ohne solche Vorwürfe und noch grössere. Nur die zehn Tage nach Ruths Geburt, glaub ich, hab ich ohne Verlust gelebt; die Wirklichkeit so unbeschreiblich findend, bis in kleinste hinein, wie sie ja wahrscheinlich immer ist." - Ruth Sieber-Rilke (ed.), Rainer Maria Rilke: Briefe aus den Jahren 1897 - 1914 (Insel-Verlag 1950), pg. 176.

[110] "Der Himmel war von weichem Grau mit wenigen hellen Spalten und Sprüngen, von denen überhellt das Land nach allen Seiten hin tief und weit war. Wie biblische Landschaften waren die Fernen mit Bergen, Baumgruppen und Wasserläufen…Einfach in der Kontur, nicht irgendeine Gegend, einfach: die Erde. Die Erde, in welche die Völker sind zerstreut worden wie Staub im Sturm. Die Erde, die dem Menschen zu gross ist, die unter seinem Wandern in die Himmel wächst und über Tage und Nächte hinaus und die jenseits der Meere immer wieder beginnt und wächst, diese biblische fremde Erde, die Erde, die Gott noch in der Hand hält und die deshalb ohne Anfang und Absehen ist. Sehr dunkel und stumpf stand die Heide da, sanft wie japanische Seide das schüttere Gras, metallisch rot das gemähte Buchweizenfeld, dunkel und schwer das umgeackerte Land." - Ruth Sieber-Rilke und Carl Sieber, Rainer Maria Rilke: Tagebücher aus der Frühzeit (Insel-Verlag 1942), pg. 337.

[111] "Schon die Wagenfahrt durch den verglasten harten Herbstnachmittag und das naive Land war so schön. Ich fuhr allein von der Bahn und zur Bahn zurück. Und das war Böhmen, das ich kannte, hügelig wie leichte Musik und auf einmal wieder eben hinter seinen Apfelbäumen, flach ohne viel Horizont und eingeteilt durch die Äcker und Baumreihen wie ein Volkslied von Refrain zu Refrain." - Ruth Sieber-Rilke (ed.), Rainer Maria Rilke: Briefe aus den Jahren 1897 - 1914 (Insel-Verlag 1950), pg. 225.

[112] "Erst muss man Gott irgendwo finden, ihn erfahren, also so unendlich, so überaus, so ungeheurer vorhanden –, dann sei's Furcht, sei's Staunen, sei's Atemlosigkeit, sei's am Ende – Liebe, was man dann zu ihm fasst, darauf kommt es kaum noch an, - aber der Glaube, dieser Zwang zu Gott, hat keinen Platz, wo einer mit der Entdeckung Gottes begonnen hat, in der es dann kein Aufhören mehr gibt, mag man an welcher Stelle immer begonnen haben." - Ruth Sieber-Rilke (ed.), Rainer Maria Rilke: Briefe aus den Jahren 1914-1926 (Insel-Verlag 1950), pg. 284.

[113] "Ach, wir rechnen die Jahre und machen Abschnitte da und dort und hören auf und fangen an und zögern zwischen beidem. Aber wie sehr ist, was uns begegnet, aus einem Stück, in welcher Verwandtschaft steht eines zum anderen, hat sich geboren und wächst heran und wird erzogen zu sich selbst, und wir haben im Grunde nur dazusein, aber schlicht, aber inständig, wie die Erde da ist, den Jahreszeiten zustimmend, hell und dunkel und ganz im Raum, nicht verlangend in anderem aufzuruhen als in dem Netz von Einflüssen und Kräften, in dem die Sterne sich sicher fühlen." - Ruth Sieber-Rilke (ed.), Rainer Maria Rilke: Briefe aus den Jahren 1897 - 1914 (Insel-Verlag 1950), pg. 209.

[114] "Man muss nie verzweifeln, wenn einem etwas verloren geht, ein Mensch oder eine Freude oder ein Glück; es kommt alles noch herrlicher wieder. Was abfallen muss, fällt ab; was zu uns gehört, bleibt bei uns, denn es geht alles nach Gesetzen vor sich, die grösser als unsere Einsicht sind und mit denen wir nur scheinbar im Widerspruch stehen. Man muss in sich selber leben und an das ganze Leben denken, an alle seine Millionen Möglichkeiten, Weiten und Zukünfte, denen gegenüber es nichts Vergangenes und Verlorenes gibt." - Ruth Sieber-Rilke (ed.), Rainer Maria Rilke: Briefe aus den Jahren 1897 - 1914 (Insel-Verlag 1950), pp. 73-74.

[115] "…aber hier und dort sind Maler, die Motive suchen, Maler, die aus dem grossen Mosaik fünf kleine Steine herausbrechen, um sie zu einer Harmonie zusammenzustellen. Und vielleicht sind nicht nur die Maler so…vielleicht sind die Menschen überhaupt so –: haben sie nicht auch das Leben aus kleinen Motiven gemacht, sind ihre Freuden und ihre Trübsale, ihre Berufe und Reichstümer nicht nur Motive? Ach! Und das wirkliche Leben ist wie die wirkliche Welt. Und liegt wie eine Weidenwiese da, von der abends warmes Atmen kommt und

Book of Hours (Ghent, Belgium ca. 1320-1330)
Text in Latin, Flemish and French
Binding by Léon Gruel (French late 19th-early 20th centuries)
ink and pigments on parchment
bound between boards covered with velvet

Duft und Menschenlosigkeit..." - Ruth Sieber-Rilke and Carl Sieber, Rainer Maria Rilke, Briefe aus den Jahren 1902 - 1906 (Insel-Verlag 1930), pg. 207.

[116] "So ist jener schmale Jüngling, der kniet und seine Arme empor wirft und zurück in einer Geste der Anrufung ohne Grenzen. Rodin hat dies Figur *Der verlorene Sohn* genannt, aber sie hat, man weiss nicht woher, auf einmal den Namen: *Prière*. Und sie wächst auch über diesen hinaus. Das is nicht ein Sohn, der vor dem Vater kniet. Diese Gebärde macht einen Gott notwendig, und in dem, der sie tut, sind alle, die ihn brauchen. Diesem Stein gehören alle Weiten; er ist allein auf der Welt." Ernst Zinn (editor), Rainer Maria Rilke Sämtliche Werke in Zwölf Bänden, Band 9 (Insel-Verlag 1975), pp. 194-195.

[117] "Ich werf es alles modernen Religionen vor, dass sie ihren Gläubigen Tröstungen und Beschönigungen des Todes geliefert haben, statt ihnen Mittel ins Gemüt zu geben, sich mit ihm zu vertragen und zu verständigen. Mit ihm, mit seiner völligen, unmaskierten Grausamkeit: diese Grausamkeit ist so ungeheurer, dass sich gerade bei ihr der Kreis schliesst...wie der Mond, so hat gewiss das Leben eine uns dauernd abgewendete Seite, die nicht sein Gegenteil ist, sonder seine Ergänzung zur Vollkommenheit, zur Vollzähligkeit, zu der wirklichen heilen und vollen Sphäre und Kugel des Seins...Nur weil wir den Tod ausschliessen in einer plötzlichen Besinnung, ist er mehr und mehr zum Fremden geworden, und da wir ihn in Fremden hielten, ein Feindliches...Das Leben sagt immer zugleich: Ja und Nein. Er, der Tod...is der eigentliche Ja-Sager. Er sagt nur: Ja. Vor der Ewigkeit." - Ruth Sieber-Rilke (ed.), Rainer Maria Rilke: Briefe aus den Jahren 1914 - 1926 (Insel-Verlag 1950), pp. 380-382.

[118] "Ich erfand mir eine neue Zärtlichkeit: eine Rose leise auf das geschlossene Auge zu legen, bis sie mit ihrer Kühle kaum mehr fühlbar ist und nur die Sanftmut ihres Blattes noch über dem Lid ruht wie Schlaf vor Sonnenaufgang." - Ruth Sieber-Rilke und Carl Sieber, Rainer Maria Rilke: Tagebücher aus der Frühzeit (Insel-Verlag 1942), pg. 309.

[119] "...Meere, Parke, Wald und Waldwiesen: meine Sehnsucht nach alledem ist manchmal unbeschreiblich. Jetzt, da es hier schon mit dem Winter droht. Schon fangen die Dunst-morgen und Abende an, wo die Sonne nur noch wie die Stelle ist, wo früher die Sonne war, und wo in den Parterres alle die Sommerblumen, die Dahlien und grossen Gladiolen und die langen Reihen der Geranien den Widerspruch ihres Rots in den Nebel schreien. Mich macht das traurig. Es bringt trostlose Erinnerungen herauf, man weiss nicht warum: als ginge des Stadtsommers Musik mit einer Dissonanz aus, mit einem Aufstand aller Noten; vielleicht nur, weil man das alles schon einmal so tief in sich hineingesehen und gedeutet und mit sich verbunden hat, ohne doch es je zu machen." - Ruth Sieber-Rilke (ed.), Rainer Maria Rilke: Briefe aus den Jahren 1897 - 1914 (Insel-Verlag 1950), pg. 177.

[120] See https://www.360cities.net/image/grab-von-rilke and https://www.findagrave.com/memorial/2190/rainer-maria-rilke.

[121] "...indem nämlich aus jeder in Gebrauch genommenen Bedeutung Gott und Tod abgezogen schienen (als ein nicht Hiesiges, sondern Späteres, Anderwärtiges und Anderes), beschleunigte sich der kleinere Kreislauf des Hiesigen immer mehr, der sogenannte Fortschritt wurde zum Ereignis einer in sich befangenen Welt, die vergass, dass sie, wie sie sich auch anstellte, durch den Tod und durch Gott von vorneherein und endgültig übertroffen war. Nun hätte das noch eine Art Besinnung ergeben, wäre man imstande gewesen, Gott und Tod als blosse Ideen sich im Geistigen fernzuhalten -: aber die Natur wusste nicht nichts von dieser uns irgendwie gelungenen Verdrängung – blüht ein Baum, so blüht so gut der Tod in ihm wie das Leben, und der Acker is voller Tod, der aus seinem liegenden Gesicht einen reichen Ausdruck des Lebens treibt, und die Tiere gehen geduldig von einem [zum] anderen – und überall um uns ist der Tod noch zu Haus und aus den Ritzen der Dinge sieht er uns zu, und ein rostiger Nagel, der irgendwo aus einer Planke steht, tut Tag und Nacht nichts, als

Book of Hours (Use of Saint-Omer)
(Northeastern France, early 14th century)
ink and pigments on parchment bound
between boards covered with leather

sich freuen über ihn." - Ruth Sieber-Rilke (ed.), Rainer Maria Rilke: Briefe aus den Jahren 1914 - 1926 (Insel-Verlag 1950), pp. 55-56.

[122] "Ich möchte Dir sagen, liebe Lou, dass Paris eine ähnliche Erfahrung für mich war wie die Militär-schule; wie damals ein grosses banges Erstaunen mich ergriff, so griff mich jetzt wieder das Entsetzen an vor alledem, was, wie in einer unsäglichen Verwirrung, Leben heist. … die Wagen…machten keinen Umweg um mich und rannten voll Verachtung über mich hin wie über eine schlechte Stelle, in der altes Wasser sich gesammelt hat. Und oft vor dem Einschlafen las ich das 30. Kapitel im Buch Hiob, und es war alles wahr an mir, Wort für Wort…

Und einmal spät im Herbst stand abends eine kleine Alte neben mir im Scheine eines Schaufensters. Sie stand ganz still, und ich glaubte sie gleich mir mit der Betrachtung der ausgelegten Sachen beschäftigt und achtete ihrer kaum. Schliesslich aber fühlte ich mich von ihrer Nähe beunruhigt, und ich weiss nicht, weshalb ich plötzlich auf ihre eigentümlich zusammengelegten abgetragenen Hände sah. Ganz, ganz langsam stieg aus diesen Händen ein alter, langer, dünner Bleistift hervor, er wuchs und wuchs, und es dauerte sehr lange, bis er ganz sichtbar war, sichtbar in seinem ganz Elend. Ich kann nicht sagen, was so entsetzlich wirkte an dieser Szene, aber es war mir, als spielte sich vor mir ein ganzes Schicksal ab, ein langes Schicksal, eine Katastrophe, die sich furchtbar steigerte bis zum Augenblick, da der Bleistift nicht mehr wuchs und ganz leise zitternd herausragte aus der Einsamkeit dieser leeren Hände. Ich begriff schliesslich, dass ich ihn kaufen sollte. - Ruth Sieber-Rilke and Carl Sieber (ed.), Rainer Maria Rilke: Briefe aus den Jahren 1892-1904 (Insel-Verlag 1939), pp. 360, 363-364.

[123] "Nach dem Gehaste der Stadt wieder diesen hohen wartenden Wald zu sehen! Wie vornehm ist doch das Stehen, die Ruhe. Verwirrt von den heftigen Gesten der Menschen, fühlt man, dass es nur zwei verwandte und grosse Bewegungen gibt. Der Flügelschlag eines hohen Vogels und das Schwanken der Wipfel. Diese beiden Gebärden sollen deine Seele lehren, sich zu bewegen." - Ruth Sieber-Rilke und Carl Sieber, Rainer Maria Rilke, Tagebücher aus der Frühzeit (Insel-Verlag 1942), pp. 218-219.

[124] "Hier war ein lebensgrosser Akt, auf dessen allen Stellen das Leben nich nur gleich mächtig war, es schien auch überall zur Höhe desselben Ausdrucks erhoben zu sein…Es war, als stiege in die Adern dieses Mannes Kraft aus den Tiefen der Erde. Das war die Silhouette eines Baumes, der die Märzstürme noch vor sich hat und bange ist, weil die Frucht and Fülle seines Sommers nicht mehr in den Wurzeln wohnt, sondern schon, langsam steigend, im Stamme steht, um den die grossen Winde jagen werden. Diese Gestalt is auch noch in anderem Sinne bedeutsam. Sie bezeichnet im Werke Rodins die Geburt der Gebärde. Jene Gebärde, die wuchs und sich allmählich zu solcher Grösse und Gewalt entwickelte, hier entsprang sie wie eine Quelle, welche leise an diesem Leibe niederrann… Zögernd entfaltet sie sich in den erhobenen Armen; und diese Arme sind noch so schwer, dass die Hand des einen schon wieder ausruht auf der Höhe des Hauptes. Aber sie schläft nichtmehr, sie sammelt sich…Und in dem rechten Fusse steht wartend ein erster Schritt." - Ernst Zinn (editor), Rainer Maria Rilke Sämtliche Werke in Zwölf Bänden, Band 9 (Insel-Verlag 1975), pp. 160-161.

[125] "So kommt es, dass die meisten Menschen gar nicht wissen, wie schön die Welt ist und wieviel Pracht in den kleinsten Dingen, in irgendeiner Blume, einem Stein, einer Baumrinde oder einem Birkenblatt sich offenbart. …Und doch wäre es das Schönste, wenn alle Menschen in dieser Beziehung immer wie aufmerksame und gute Kinder bleiben wollten, einfältig und fromm im Gefühl, und wenn sie die Fähigkeit nicht verlieren würden, sich an einem Birkenblatt oder an der Feder eines Pfauen oder an der Schwinge einer Nebelkrähe so innig zu freuen wie an einem grossen Gebirge oder einem prächtigen Palast. Das Kleine ist ebensowenig klein als das Grosse – gross ist. Es geht eine grosse and ewige Schönheit durch die ganze Welt, und diese is gerecht über den kleinen und grossen Dingen verstreut; den es gibt im Wichtigen und Wesentlichen keine Ungerechtigkeit auf der

Vienna Book of Hours, non-original binding
by Abigail Quandt, Walters Art Museum (1985),
with white goatskin over wooden boards
and two woven clasps with metal fittings

ganzen Erde." – Ruth Sieber-Rilke and Carl Sieber (ed.), <u>Rainer Maria Rilke: Briefe aus den Jahren 1892-1904</u> (Insel-Verlag 1939), pg. 178.

[126] "The 'Fioretti of Saint Francis' [the <u>Little Flowers of Saint Francis</u>, a book about the disciples of Saint Francis] are old friendships for my nature, at least in their original text. Years ago, during a whole south Italian Winter, I gathered my housemates every morning about my reading aloud of these little and lovely legends; they would always listen to one selection, that sufficed to set us up for the day, each in his own way…." – RMR Letter to Ilse Blumenthal-Weiss, 25 April, 1922.

"Die 'Fioretti des heiligen Franz' sind alte Freundschaften für mein Gemüt, wenigstens in ihrem Urtext. Vor Jahren, während eines ganzen süditalienischen Winters, versammelte ich um mein Vorlesen dieser kleinen und liebevollen Legenden jeden Morgen meine Hausgenossen; sie hörten dann immer einen Abschnitt an, das reichte hin, um in den Tag, den dann jeder auf seine Weise…" – Ruth Sieber-Rilke and Carl Sieber (ed.), <u>Rainer Maria Rilke: Briefe aus Muzot 1921 - 1926</u> (Insel-Verlag 1935), pp. 130-131.

[127] "Trotzdem bin ich vielleicht schon dabei, mein Leben begonnen zu haben; jenes, das man nicht mehr loslässt, ehe man es vollendet hat; es sei den, dass man über dieser ehrlichen Arbeit stirbt; aber dann kommt dieses Leben, das man dennoch zu eigen besass, über einen anderen oder über eine Landschaft oder über Gott. Hast du es erst einmal bis zu einem gewissen Punkte geführt, dann vollendet es sich um jeden Preis – ob in deiner Gegenwart, oder später – wer bangt darum?" - Ruth Sieber-Rilke und Carl Sieber, <u>Rainer Maria Rilke: Tagebücher aus der Frühzeit</u> (Insel-Verlag 1942), pp. 154-155.

[128] "Jetzt waren alle auf den dunklen Vorplatz getreten, dessen Mauerrand weich und weiss um die Nacht sich schlang. Und plötzlich – täuscht mich der Wind? – Stimmen, leise, wachsend, nicht wie anfangende, einsetzende Stimmen, wie Stimmen mitten in einem Lied, das immer ist und das nur denen, die im Innern sehr stille werden, auf einmal vernehmbar gegeben wird, und ich höre: 'Ehre sei Gott in der Höhe…' Und da wusste ich, das gerade dieses wie über viele Stufen steigende Lied immer ist und das es uns bewusst wird, wenn wir singende Profile sehen vor Sternennächten." - Ruth Sieber-Rilke und Carl Sieber, <u>Rainer Maria Rilke: Tagebücher aus der Frühzeit</u> (Insel-Verlag 1942), pg. 347.

"Dog Chasing Hare", Marginalia from Leaf of Office of the Dead, Book of Hours (France, 14th century)

www.ingramcontent.com/pod-product-compliance
Lightning Source LLC
Chambersburg PA
CBHW042130010526
44111CB00032B/67